Slandering the angels

SLANDERING THE ANGELS

The message of Jude

John Benton

EVANGELICAL PRESS

EVANGELICAL PRESS
Grange Close, Faverdale North Industrial Estate, Darlington, DL3
0PH, England

First published 1999

British Library Cataloguing in Publication Data available

ISBN 0 85234 424 4

Printed and bound in Great Britain by Creative Print and Design
Wales, Ebbw Vale

To Josiah Ogalo Agengo,
a faithful pastor of God's flock.

'There is nothing more tedious
than the continuous search for novelty'
(Garrison Keiller)

Contents

Preface

This book began life as a series of messages delivered in the summer of 1996 to a group of pastors and their wives of the African Inland Church. The leaders had asked me to open up the epistle of Jude. The conference took place out in the rural areas of Western Kenya, where the struggle with poverty and with superstition is continual. There, under the corrugated iron roof, in the very simple quarters of the newly built library at Nyakach Girls School, we enjoyed exploring the Scriptures together.

I had preached through Jude some years before, but decided that I must make a completely fresh start on the letter if I was going to be of any use to these valiant brothers and sisters who labour for the Lord under such difficult conditions. Time was short and I had not really completed my preparations on the epistle when we got there. But each morning as I arose, the Lord seemed to shed fresh light on this letter and fresh life into the preacher. Sharing the conference with me were my wife Ann and two elders and their wives from our congregation. They are Pablo and Penny Fernandez and Marcus and Jennifer Watkins. My youngest son Owen also came along. I think we can all say that this visit to Kenya, though not always easy, was one of the most blessed experiences of our Christian lives. The sense of the Lord's hand upon us was almost tangible.

On our return from Kenya, the text of the messages on Jude went through a further revision as I used them as Bible addresses for an autumn series of Sunday evening services at Chertsey Street Baptist Church in Guildford. It was a time at which the 'Toronto Blessing' was still at its height in our area and the messages from Jude, I hope, helped us all to get things in perspective. We all want to see true revival visit our land, but are very wary of what is spurious, even when it is perpetrated by good Christian people whose hearts are in the right place. That autumn was also a time during which the ongoing struggle for biblical standards of sexual behaviour in the church was being fought out. Many who are able to grab the attention of the media are arguing that the church should forget what they see as the old-fashioned taboos of the past and embrace the 'sexual revolution'. Again, Jude helped us to see that this is no new struggle and that true spirituality always walks hand in hand with biblical holiness.

It is with a sense of God having used this material for good in the past that it is now made available through this Welwyn Commentary. I trust and pray that the Lord will show his smiling face and his astounding graciousness through these pages.

I am glad to express my ongoing thanks to the people and leaders of the Chertsey Street fellowship in Guildford, who are my family whom I love in the Lord. I must also express my thanks to Liz Crawley at the offices of *Evangelicals Now* who worked copying messages from audio tapes on to floppy disks so that I might have an easier time writing up the material.

John Benton
March 1999

Introduction

It is often the peculiarities and perceived difficulties of a New Testament letter which provide the key to a deeper grasp of its message. The particular background to which the letter was addressed can sometimes emerge into clearer focus from a study of the unusual details and so facilitate a sharper application of the text. This is the case with the short epistle of Jude, the penultimate book in our Bibles.

Looking at this letter through modern eyes, we are struck by a number of rare features. Perhaps the most obvious is the close similarity between Jude and 2 Peter. At first glance the parallel seems so close that we might wonder why Jude's letter was necessary at all. It seems almost to be a duplicate of a large section of Peter's material.

Then the next thing which strikes us as strange is Jude's near obsession with angels. Celestial spirits are, of course, referred to elsewhere in the New Testament. But in this short letter of just twenty-five verses, there are at least four separate references to angelic beings (vv. 6,8,9,14). 'Why this preoccupation?' we wonder.

A further peculiarity, which particularly jars in the minds of evangelical Christians, is the fact that twice Jude quotes from extra-biblical books. In verse 9, he alludes to what scholars say is the lost ending to an inter-testamental book called *The*

Assumption of Moses. Later, in verses 14 and 15, he cites the beginning of a similar work, this time *The Book of Enoch*. These books were probably written some time during the second or first century before Christ, and were in circulation among the Jewish communities of New Testament times. Though Jude quotes from them, the church has always rejected them from inclusion within the canon of Scripture. The question arises: 'Why has Jude chosen to use these works?'

Then there are some lesser oddities in the book which are worth registering. Jude uses the Greek word *despotes* to describe the Lord Jesus Christ (v. 4). Though this is used of God elsewhere, and though it is an entirely appropriate word for Christ, meaning 'Master' or 'Sovereign', in the New Testament it is only used as a title for Jesus here and in the parallel passage in 2 Peter 2:1. Further, here in Jude (though not in 2 Peter), the Lord Jesus is spoken of as the *only* Sovereign. The uniqueness of Christ is very relevant to us in our increasingly pluralistic society, but why does Jude pick up on it? Do these facts give some clue as to the error which Jude is opposing?

Another unusual feature is the doxology which closes the letter. While very much in line with the New Testament doctrine of the pre-existence of Christ, it is peculiar that Jude ascribes glory to God through Jesus Christ 'before all ages' as well as now and into the eternal future (v. 25). These too are aspects of the letter which leave us wondering, 'Why?'

The general background

Bearing these thoughts in our minds, we shall first sketch out the plain thrust of Jude's epistle. It is a letter, like most New Testament letters, written to oppose certain false teachers

(vv. 4,8,10,11,12-13,16,18,19). The job of opposing error is ever necessary and actually this in particular is a mark of a good shepherd of God's flock. Even the hired hand is happy to feed the sheep; it is when the wolf comes that it is seen who are the true shepherds and who are not (John 10:11-13). Jude feels he must urgently warn Christians and the churches against following these false teachers. He sums up their error as he describes them as 'godless men, who change the grace of our God into a licence for immorality and deny Jesus Christ our only Sovereign and Lord' (v. 4).

Where did the false teachers get their teaching? Jude describes them as 'these dreamers' (v. 8). It would appear that they claimed to have received special authoritative revelation from God in dream-like experiences and visions. This claimed revelation was either to be added to the apostolic faith of Scripture, or even to supersede it. Jude's concern is that the churches should hold on to the fact that the true faith has already been 'once for all delivered to the saints', and therefore the claims of the false teachers are to be rejected and contended against.

The ethical content of the false teaching was such as to legitimize immorality of the worst sort among Christians. This is implied by the kind of examples which Jude uses to warn the churches in verses 5-7. Individual Christians and churches who are lured into such sinful lifestyles bring down the judgement of God upon themselves. By contrast, Jude's readers are encouraged to keep themselves in the love of God by prayer and obedience. The doctrinal element associated with this immorality appears to impugn the uniqueness of Christ as our *only* Sovereign and Lord.

This, then, is the general situation which the letter addresses. But how do the peculiarities of the epistle which we noted earlier relate to all this? Can we fit the details together? Can they throw any extra light on the background to Jude?

The delusion of élitism

From time to time in Christian history there have arisen those
within the church who get the idea that somehow they are a
special group who are superior to other believers. They see
themselves as a super-spiritual élite chosen by God, to whom
the guidelines of Scripture for Christian behaviour do not necessarily apply. Their claims are often backed up with prophetic
utterances and claimed instances of the miraculous. Endowed
with some extraordinary anointing of spiritual power, they feel
that they are free to indulge in practices which are contrary to
traditional Christian lifestyle. They are in a class of their own
and the normal guidelines do not apply to them.

For example, during the Civil War years of seventeenth-
century England, a number of religious groups arose who threw
aside Christian sexual norms. Christopher Hill, in his classic
introduction to the religious turmoil of the period, *The World
Turned Upside Down*, mentions a number of such sects: 'The
myth of the Everlasting Gospel goes back at least to Joachim
of Fiore in the twelfth century. This divided human history
into three ages: that of the Father, from the Fall to the death of
Christ, the age of the Law; followed by that of the Son, the
age of the Gospel; the third age, the age of the Spirit, was
always the present age, in which the Holy Spirit was coming
into the hearts of all men to free them from existing forms and
ordinances.'[1] 'Elizabethan Familists divorced, as they married,
by simple declaration before the congregation. Before 1640
such customs had been concealed... But during the Revolution they were practised and defended in public.'[2] There is
reasonable documentation that the Ranters taught 'that for
one man to be tied to one woman, or one woman to one man,
is a fruit of the curse; but, they say, we are freed from the
curse, therefore it is our liberty to make use of whom we
please'.[3] The idea of God's free grace and the Spirit bringing
freedom has often been used as a cover for sin by radical groups.

Today there are those in some extreme charismatic circles who look for God to raise up a 'new breed' of Christian. This new breed, it is said, will be anointed and empowered by the Spirit in a remarkable way to be an invincible end-time army for the Lord. They will be on a different level from ordinary Christian people. It is just such groups, which see themselves as a spiritual élite, receiving new revelation from God over and above the Scriptures, who are vulnerable to the delusion that normal Christian morality no longer applies to them and their followers.

In the broader religious world we can think of the New Age movement which has arisen in the West in the last thirty years. This mixture of Eastern spirituality and occult ideas has been termed a return to paganism.[4] It is a spirituality of self-fulfilment and its literature encourages its devotees to see themselves as 'gods'. There is a rejection of traditional ideas of morality in favour of the ethics of emotion and of the moment. With self as 'god', this movement is able to embrace promiscuous heterosexual behaviour, homosexuality and lesbianism as valid expressions of spirituality. Many churches and church bodies are openly being influenced by this movement.

Certainly we are told that the false teachers opposed by Jude were boastful (v. 16) and saw themselves as above authority (v. 8), and it seems to me that if they are located somewhere in this kind of spiritually élitist category, then many of the questions raised by the peculiarities of the letter can be given reasonable answers.

A possible scenario

Certainty is not possible, but it appears that the following scenario makes a lot of sense.

The false teachers referred to by Jude saw themselves as having received special revelation from God (v. 8), which was

subsequent to, and went beyond, the apostolic faith (v. 4). The
dreams and visions they claimed to have had involved contact
with angels and other celestial beings, and as a result they
were given understanding into supposed new truth concerning the spiritual realm and God's will for this world. These
false teachers probably saw themselves as having been raised
by the grace of God to a higher spiritual status, and as being
on a par with angels, or even above them. They may even
have claimed to have undergone some transformation which
made them akin to celestial beings, rather like the stories put
around by those in our own day who claim to have been ab-
ducted by aliens and undergone some modification, such as an
implant in their bodies which makes them more than human.
Since the apostle Paul speaks of Christians judging angels in
the world to come (1 Cor. 6:3), their ideas can be thought of
in terms of over-realized eschatology, or claiming to experience now something which has yet to be fulfilled in the future.
They claimed to be able to move in a dimension as yet inac-
cessible to the ordinary believer.

This idea may seem fantastic to us, but in the widely circulated *Book of Enoch*, from which Jude quotes, the patriarch
Enoch is depicted as a godly man who has many visions of
angels and is let into celestial secrets while journeying in the
spiritual dimension. Such ideas, then, would not seem unusual
to many first-century Jewish people who had been touched by
the gospel. At least at one point in the *Book of Enoch*, the
patriarch is described as acting as an intermediary between
rebellious angels and God himself. Similarly *The Assumption
of Moses* is another book of supposed prophetical history in
which information is purportedly given in the ending concerning action between celestial beings.

These ideas, as I say, may seem fantastic to us and yet in
our own day New Age devotees claim to have had similar
experiences. Again, sections of wider evangelicalism, such as

the health and prosperity churches, which have been influenced by New Age ideas, ply congregations with similar stories. Of course, the Roman Catholic Church has throughout history embraced those who have reported they have had strange visions of angels, or of the virgin Mary, and claimed to have received messages and extraordinary powers. Indeed, they have often gone on to designate such people as an élite group of 'saints'.

Allying themselves with experiences similar to the adventures of Enoch, the false teachers may have attached the term 'masters' *(despotes)* to themselves (v. 4), or even have seen themselves as in some sense 'gods'. With supposed power over angels, we can imagine many embroidered stories littering their racy sermons to gullible congregations in which they boasted of treating angels as servants, and casting out demonic spirits with abusive language (v. 8). Such stories of dazzling spiritual prowess would have made heady illustrations of their doctrine and produced a huge impact on their listeners, just as such stories continue to do in many circles today. 'How can we gainsay such men who have had such remarkable experiences?' would be the thought in the minds of many believers. And when such stories are used to legitimize the throwing off of restraint which fallen and corrupt human nature craves, this becomes a potent force indeed. The congregation is not only mentally excited; the flesh is hearing what it has always wanted to hear.

If this is somewhere near the true background against which Jude is writing, it would provide a straightforward reason as to why he would choose to quote from *The Assumption of Moses* and the *Book of Enoch*. If the false teachers were claiming revelation on a par with, or superseding, Scripture and the revelation through the Lord Jesus, then, initially at least, Jude must find ways of arguing against them other than reference to Christ and his apostles. Thus Jude chooses to base much of his case on inter-testamental literature. The point would be, not that these documents were necessarily authoritative, but that they reject sin and command godliness. The line of Jude's argument would be simple. Here are documents which parallel the supposed experiences of the false teachers and which they may well have used to some extent to substantiate their claims, but these very same documents contradict their lax morality. Jude would be answering the claims of the false teachers from their own preferred material. We can understand, then, why Jude would quote these books without in any way having to revise the traditional view about the canon of Scripture.

Why Jude writes

Further, this idea of an élite group claiming angelic visitations may well hold the key as to why Jude felt it necessary to write his letter, even though it is so close in content to 2 Peter. Some scholars have argued that Jude in fact acted as the secretary to Peter, writing down Peter's thoughts to form his second letter.[5] This would certainly account for Jude's familiarity with the 2 Peter material. But why would Jude himself feel that he must put pen to paper in his own name?

If Jude had been closely involved with the apostle in writing 2 Peter, and also was aware that what had been prophesied as still being in the future in 2 Peter 2:1 ('There will be false teachers among you [who] will secretly introduce destructive heresies, even denying the sovereign Lord who bought them') had now actually come to pass, then this may well have stirred him to feel that he had a particular obligation to write to the churches.

But perhaps the answer lies more particularly in the fact that, as we shall argue later, Jude was a part of the earthly family of the Lord Jesus Christ, a child of Mary and Joseph, a brother of James (v. 1) and a half-brother of the Lord Jesus.

In his commentary on Jude, Richard Bauckham points out that, according to Julius Africanus, who lived in Emmaus in the late second century, members of the family of Jesus were known as the *desposunoi*. This is related to the idea that the Lord Jesus was known as *ho despotes,* the Master, in early Palestinian Christian circles in which his family was known. If this was the case, it indicates that the family was popularly regarded as a special group. Certainly it was a family, the father and mother of which had truly been visited by angels in connection with the nativity of Jesus. Yet Jude, in his letter opposing élitist false teachers, calls himself only a 'servant' of Jesus Christ. The point would be this: if Jude, who was popularly seen as belonging to the élite comprised by the earthly family of Jesus, will only call himself a 'servant' of Jesus Christ, what right do these (false) teachers have to see themselves as masters? This would have particular force coming from someone like Jude, rather than, say, Peter, who was not a part of the so-called 'holy family'. If our scenario is somewhere near the truth, it may have been such a consideration that moved Jude himself to write.

The wider question

There is a sense in which every group of false teachers sees itself as an élite. They see themselves as having the crucial truth, whereas others, only going by the Scriptures, are living in darkness. They may teach that such ordinary Christians are not really believers at all; since they have not experienced the particular emphasis of the false teachers, all their Christianity is deemed invalid. However, Jude's false teachers do not seem to have been of this kind. Usually such teachers form their own groups outside the umbrella of the church. They become sects. By contrast, Jude's false teachers were quite willing to join in the love feasts and communion services of the church

(v. 12). Jude expressly describes them as having 'secretly slipped in among you' (v. 4). They were not seeking overtly to divide the church and take a group right out of it; rather it seems they were trying to subvert the whole church from the inside. In many ways this is far more dangerous than the strategy of sectarians.

Their line to ordinary believers presumably would have been in terms of saying, 'Yes, we accept that you are Christian, *but you are not Christian enough.* Our teaching, and the experiences we can lead you into, will alone make you fully Christian. You are not as free as you could be in Christ.'

Of course, our Christian lives can always be improved, and there is always a sense in which we can all become more fully Christian. But any such 'improvement' which steps outside the bounds of the scriptural faith once for all delivered to God's people, and which makes sin an acceptable part of supposed Christian living, is to be avoided and rejected.

It is not just through claimed charismatic experience that people can set themselves up as an élite. There are many other ways of doing the same thing. Intellectual attainment can also be used as the building material for a two-tier Christianity. Then again, it may be that being brought up in a certain doctrinal tradition will encourage some to see themselves as somehow superior to other Christians. We will bear such tendencies in mind as we try to give application to the wider sweep of what Jude has to say to us as Christians.

1. Christopher Hill, *The World Turned Upside Down,* Penguin, 1991, pp.147-8.
2. As above, p.311.
3. As above, p.318.
4. See Peter Jones, *Spirit Wars: Pagan revival in Christian America*, Winepress Publishers, 1997.
5. See J. A. T. Robinson, *Redating the New Testament,* SCM, 1977.

1.
In the family

Please read Jude 1-2

At the turn of the second millennium, as faithful Christians in the West watch and pray for the coming of the kingdom of God, on the surface there is much to depress us. Biblical truth is opposed both outside and inside the church. The latest false teachings seem to sweep through the church and often appear to be on the verge of taking over. Worldliness and moral laxity have become an increasing problem for the church.

Meanwhile, the true gospel is derided as small-minded, shabby and outmoded by the theological pace-setters of the academy. The entrepreneurs and prophets of show-business religion look down on it as 'traditional' and unexciting. The neo-pagan purveyors of strange religious experiences spurn it as unspiritual. The influential dignitaries of the church distance themselves from it in an attempt to keep a good media image. At the same time the arrogant secular world disdains the good news of sins forgiven and eternal life in Jesus Christ as an insignificant, out-of-date myth — foolish nonsense which adult people should have outgrown long ago. The majority in both the professing church and the unbelieving world prefer new and more 'enlightened' approaches to salvation and lifestyle. Traditionally, Jude is known as the patron saint of lost causes and sometimes the gospel itself can seem like a lost cause.

But, according to Jesus, the majority is always wrong on such matters: 'Small is the gate and narrow the road that leads to life, and only a few find it' (Matt. 7:14). For those who find it, this small gate, this despised gospel, really does lead to life: 'It is the power of God for the salvation of everyone who believes' (Rom. 1:16).

Heresies

Jude is writing to Christian believers at a time when the gospel is under attack from false teachers who have infiltrated among them: 'I felt I had to write and urge you to contend for the faith that was once for all entrusted to the saints. For certain men whose condemnation was written about long ago have secretly slipped in among you' (vv. 3-4). The scenario here could refer to churches generally where false teaching had gained influence. Or it may refer to just one local church where this has happened and which was particularly well known to Jude. Either way, Jude is writing to combat this influx of heresy which he sees overwhelming and endangering the people of God. The most important features of the heresy are that it constitutes an attack on the moral purity of the church and the doctrinal truth about Jesus Christ. The heretics 'change the grace of our God into a licence for immorality and deny Jesus Christ our only Sovereign and Lord' (v. 4).

We have already given some thought in the introduction to the possible nature of the heresy which Jude is addressing. But suffice it to say that these main elements of morality and Christology seem linked into an interest in angelic spirits which permeates the whole epistle. For a New Testament letter as short as Jude's, the number of references to celestial beings is quite disproportionate. We will do our best to see how this interest fits into the jigsaw.

The issues of truth and moral integrity are fundamental to the health and vitality of the church. To drift in these areas is to put in jeopardy the church's very existence. This should ring alarm bells for the church, especially in the contemporary Western world. We are surrounded by a culture of ever more serious moral decadence, where the concept of truth itself is under increasing attack. There are immense and subtle pressures on the church to compromise in these vital areas. The letter of Jude could not be more pertinent to us.

It is a short letter, only twenty-five verses. But it is extremely potent. Think of a tiny dose of penicillin which can heal a person of a deadly disease. Think of a small personal computer which can carry vast amounts of vital information. Think of the mighty Goliath, felled with one little stone. In the providence of God this diminutive letter can heal sick churches, inform and clarify the thinking of God's people at a vital time and slay giant threats to the spiritual lives of Christians.

Jude's attitude

It is worth noticing two things about heresy generally before we proceed.

First, we can immediately detect that Jude's attitude is clearly out of step with that of the modern world and its dominant philosophy. Even though he is a man of love who would far rather have been able to write a non-controversial letter (v. 3), his concern for truth would be viewed today as an anachronism. Our age is in the process of abandoning the notion of objective truth, especially in matters of faith and spirituality.

So-called 'post-modernism' and the New Age movement are increasingly influencing our culture and they are two sides of the same coin. The New Age movement tells people they have the power within them to shape their own reality. Post-modernism tells people that reality is only what they subjectively perceive it to be. Either way, with the concept of men and women shaping reality or perceiving reality, truth is a fluid commodity, malleable in the hands of human beings.

Then again, globalization is on the world agenda. The spirit of our times is one of multi-faith and multiculturalism which insists that no one religion can claim to have the truth. We all wish to see peace on earth. But for the sake of peace between people, our society brands all attempts to argue the truth of any religion as bigotry and demands that every opinion be treated as equally valid. Jude's statement that Jesus Christ is our '*only* Sovereign and Lord' (v. 4) does not sit easily with the spirit of our age.

The only heresy for the contemporary world is to say that there is such a thing as heresy. 'All opinions are valid.' 'All faiths lead to God.' 'Each one can find his own path up the same mountain.' Such slogans as these rule contemporary society.

But our author would disagree. For Jude there is truth and error. There are such things as false teachers. Though authentic Christianity is spacious and does not restrict all Christians to seeing everything in precisely the same way, and though it makes allowances for differences of background and culture, yet there are well-defined limits. The fundamental facts concerning God, sin, and Christ and his atonement are universal and absolute. This truth, revealed by God, Jude calls 'the faith'. We can step out of truth and into error. There are true Christians and there are heretics. But for heretics and their followers, says Jude, 'blackest darkness has been reserved for ever' (v. 13). To be a false teacher, or to follow one, is to be lost.

We need to be clear as to what is at stake here. Jesus said, 'I am the way and the truth and the life. No one comes to the Father except through me' (John 14:6). If contemporary society is right when it tells us there is no truth and that all paths lead to God, then the Lord Jesus was wrong. This is not a matter of insignificance to the church! It is a matter of momentous proportions. In fact there is no evidence at all that the 'All religions lead to God' theory current in our society is true. Different religions are so contradictory that one can only hold to the theory by abandoning the very idea of truth itself. To abandon the categories of truth and error is to abandon Christianity for a diametrically opposed world-view. The issue of truth is crucial.

Secondly, as we consider heresy generally, at the outset of looking at Jude's letter we need to notice something else. Jude calls us to 'contend for the faith that was once for all entrusted to the saints', and it is as well to understand that there is more than one way of departing from the body of salvation truth that Jude calls 'the faith'. We can either subtract from it, or seek to add to it. We meet both these avenues of heresy in the New Testament. In 1 Corinthians we meet those who deny the resurrection. In 2 Peter we meet those who scoff at the truth of Christ's second coming. These people are subtracting from the faith. They thereby deny the reliability of Christ and the apostolic witness to him. By contrast, in Galatians we are confronted by those who say that we need Christ plus adherence to Jewish customs. In Colossians we meet those who would place Christ alongside other spiritual beings and powers. These people are adding to the faith. They thereby deny the all-sufficiency of Christ our Saviour.

Today, there are many false ideas. There are many suggestions as to how the church should 'improve' on the old biblical gospel in the modern age. Jude is the small but powerful antidote to such things. It is strong medicine. For this small letter is not simply the word of men, but the Word of God.

So we look at the opening two verses of this New Testament letter. They tell us about the letter's correspondents. A letter conveys a message between two parties. Who are these people? What can we learn about them for our edification? So we now ask two questions: 'Who is Jude?' and, 'Who are the recipients?'

Who is Jude?

'Jude, a servant of Jesus Christ and a brother of James.'
There is only one Jude in Scripture who has a brother named James. This is the Jude, or Judas, who was part of the earthly family of the Lord Jesus Christ. He is mentioned in Mark 6:3, when the people of his home town took offence at Jesus, saying, 'Where did this man get these things? ... Isn't this Mary's son and the brother of James, Joseph, *Judas* and Simon?' (see also the parallel passage in Matthew 13:55). The writer of this epistle is probably this same man, who had been brought up alongside Jesus.

Many modern scholars try to argue that this is only who the writer of the letter *claimed* to be. They say that in fact it was written by some other anonymous Christian who simply used Jude's name in order to lend more weight to his letter. The technical term for this is 'pseudepigraphy'. But such ideas should be viewed with great suspicion by Bible-believing Christians as, not to put too fine a point on it, this would mean that this letter which calls others to contend for the truth would itself be based on a lie.

It should also be rejected on the grounds that arguments in favour of pseudepigraphy lack cogency.

Firstly, we have already noted the very close similarity between 2 Peter and this epistle of Jude. If 2 Peter was already in circulation among the churches, as the quotation in verse 18 of 2 Peter 3:3 implies, what would be the point of an anonymous Christian's writing a letter which so closely follows Peter's work?

Secondly, scholars who argue for pseudepigraphy put forward the idea that it was a well-known and perfectly acceptable way of writing in the early days of Christianity. But the flaw in this idea is seen as we read Paul's comments in 2 Thessalonians about those who have circulated letters under his name. There were people who put around letters using Paul's name and caused great mischief by so doing (2 Thess. 2:2). Paul's reaction was not to condone the practice, but to try to ensure that the churches knew how to identify letters which had genuinely come from him (2 Thess. 3:17). We can properly surmise that Paul viewed such lack of integrity with horror.

That the writer was Jude, a half-brother to Jesus, is the best explanation of the two phrases in his introduction.

He calls himself **'a servant of Jesus Christ'**. The brothers of Jesus were not generally known as 'apostles' in the early church. So Jude simply calls himself a 'servant'. The second phrase identifies Jude as the **'brother of James'**. There is only one person in the New Testament church whom everyone would know as just 'James' without any ambiguity, and that was James the brother of Jesus (Gal. 1:19).

In these family links we can see much to encourage us at a practical level. Many of us have close family and other relatives to whom we have been witnessing for years, and yet they are still not saved. This can drive us to despair. 'Why can't they see it?' 'Is there something wrong with my Christianity?' We may ask ourselves such questions. We may feel ourselves to be total failures because our family have not come to Christ. But Jude and James provide encouragement for us. After all, these two, along with other half-brothers and half-sisters of Jesus, lived in the same house with, and grew up alongside, Jesus. Yet, living alongside God incarnate himself, they were unconverted for years. 'For even his own brothers did not believe in him' (John 7:5). Do your best to live lovingly and consistently for Christ, but don't blame yourself if your loved ones are not yet saved. People's hearts are hard. The devil has sadly blinded the minds of unbelievers (2 Cor. 4:4) and it takes the miracle of new creation to enable them to see the truth.

It was not until after Christ's death and the infallible proof of the resurrection that Jude and his brothers and sisters came to faith. It is only after the Lord Jesus had risen and ascended into heaven that we find the members of his family gathered for prayer with Christ's disciples (Acts 1:14).

Jude was unconverted for years. Though the Lord Jesus had turned the water into wine at the family wedding at Cana, though he had healed the sick and fed the thousands, none of this had touched Jude's heart and brought salvation. Somehow he had explained it all away. It may be the same with you. Your family do see that there is something different about you. They may even envy you the peace and joy which you know as you walk consistently with God. They may have a hidden regard for the guidance and certainty you have about your life. They may even half mean it when they say from time to time, 'I wish I had your faith.' Yet they put it all down to factors other than the power of God's Spirit. They put it down to 'luck', or your personality, or to 'psychology'.

But eventually Jude was converted. Eventually the evidence of the life of Jesus did begin to weigh with him. Eventually God did work in his life through the family crisis of Jesus' death and the marvellous miracle of his resurrection. In that there is encouragement for those of us with unconverted loved ones to keep praying and keep witnessing. Do not give up. Do not despair. We cannot know for certain that our families will be saved. But the Lord does say to us, 'Let us not become weary in doing good, for at the proper time we will reap a harvest if we do not give up' (Gal. 6:9). The brothers of Christ were eventually born again.

But then another question may occur to us. If Jude is the half-brother of the Lord Jesus Christ, why doesn't he say so straight out? We wonder why he does not say this, but James does not say it either at the beginning of his New Testament letter. The answer is probably twofold.

First, Jude recognizes that *physical ties of blood and genetics are of no eternal worth*. Spiritual ties with Jesus are what saves us. It is faith which trusts and submits to Jesus as his *servant* which unites us to the Saviour. The Lord Jesus had spelled this out during his ministry in a way which was so blunt as perhaps to cause offence to his family. Amid the pressure and controversy of his ministry in Galilee, Mark's Gospel tells of one day on which Jesus' family arrived at the crowded house where he was teaching: 'Standing outside, they sent someone in to call him. A crowd was sitting around him, and they told him, "Your mother and brothers are outside looking for you." "Who are my mother and my brothers?" he asked. Then he looked at those seated in a circle around him and said, "Here are my mother and my brothers! Whoever does God's will is my brother and sister and mother"' (Mark 3:32-35).

Second, it is not only the priority of spiritual ties which shapes how Jude introduces himself; *humility* is also involved. Humility forbids Jude from mentioning himself as a physical half-brother of Jesus. Joseph was Jude's father, but it was by the power of the Holy Spirit that the child Jesus was conceived in Mary's womb. Jesus is the eternal Son of God become a man. Knowing that Jesus is Lord and God, Jude does not want to give any impression of being equal with Jesus. Announcing himself as being from the same family as Christ could be misunderstood in such a way and Jude wishes to avoid that. So he just calls himself 'a servant of Jesus Christ and a brother of James'. Furthermore, as I have suggested in

the introduction, if the heretics in view in this epistle saw themselves as an élite group boasting of their supposed authority,
then again it is the humility of Jude, a member of Jesus' earthly
family, which would carry particular weight with Jude's readers as he writes to oppose them.

But here too in Jude's family connection with the Lord Jesus
Christ we can find wonderful encouragement in our faith. The
holy Son of God did not falter from coming alongside sinners.

It is very instructive to look at the family tree of Jesus.
Matthew begins his Gospel by delineating Christ's anteced-
ents through Joseph. He starts the genealogy with Abraham,
the father of the Jewish nation. Yet as he records the first four
names in that family tree we are reminded of the kind of family
into which Christ was born. The genealogy opens with
Abraham, Isaac, Jacob and Judah.

Abraham had been an idolater and even after God called
him his faith often failed, as, for example, when he chose to
have a son by the maid of Sarah his wife rather than to believe
God's promise of a son through Sarah herself. Abraham's God-
given son Isaac was ruled by his appetite for food and so
showed foolish favouritism to one of his sons who was a hunter,
thus bringing deep division into their family (Gen. 25:28). His
son Jacob, the third in line, deceived his brother Esau out of
his birthright. Then comes Jacob's son Judah who, among other
things, got his daughter-in-law Tamar pregnant. An idolater, a
failed father, a liar and an adulterer — and they are just the
first four in the family tree. What a family! Yet into such a
family the Lord Jesus Christ, our Saviour, was pleased to be
born as a great sign of his solidarity with sinners like ourselves. We can feel so unworthy and guilty in our sinfulness
that sometimes we cannot understand how the Son of God
would ever want us. Yet such facts in relation to Christ's family underline the promise that he made: 'Whoever comes to
me I will never drive away' (John 6:37). Jude himself had

rejected Jesus for years and yet Jesus did not reject him. The astonishing truth of the gospel is that God actually does love sinners.

Who are the recipients?

But, turning from the writer, let us look at those to whom Jude's letter is addressed. Jude describes his readers in the following words: **'To those who have been called, who are loved by God the Father and kept by Jesus Christ.'**
You will notice that Jude uses a triplet in his description here. His readers are 'called', 'loved' and 'kept'. As we proceed through Jude's letter we shall see that he likes the number three. He uses threesomes on many occasions. In verse 2 he greets his readers with a threesome, 'mercy, peace and love'. When, in verses 5-7, he speaks of God's judgement, he gives three examples: those who died in the desert after the Exodus, the fallen angels and the destruction of Sodom and Gomorrah. When, in verse 11, he speaks of false teachers, he gives a trio of Old Testament examples: Cain, Balaam and Korah. There are other threesomes as well for which you might like to look out as we proceed.

As Jude describes the recipients of his letter he is really answering the crucial foundational question: 'What is a Christian?' We have already begun to touch on the marvel of salvation. We have already seen that it is spiritual ties to Christ, rather than ties of flesh and blood, which are vital. But what is it that makes a Christian? As the church is confronted by false teaching this is a crucial question. Jude uses three wonderful words.

A Christian is not simply someone who attends church. A Christian is certainly not just anyone who is born of Christian parents, or happens to have been born in a 'Christian' country.

Neither is a Christian simply someone who seeks to be kind to others and tries to live by the 'golden rule'. There is nothing wrong with being kind. It is to be encouraged. But there are many kind atheists or Buddhists. It is not kindness which makes a Christian. In particular, in the context of the sort of error Jude is confronting, the churches need reminding that a Christian is not someone who has simply had some vivid spiritual experience or other. Jude tells us that a Christian is someone who is 'called', 'loved' and 'kept' (v. 1).

Called by God

First, a Christian is someone who has been **'called'** by God (v. 1). In the Old Testament, Israel is described, especially by Isaiah, as having been called to be God's servant (Isa. 41:9; 42:6). Similarly, the Christian is one who has been called by God. Through the gospel of Christ, maybe in a meeting or through the personal witness of a friend, all true Christians have heard the voice of God speaking to them in the depth of their souls. They have heard the Holy Spirit calling them away from this world and its fading pleasures. They have felt him convicting them of their sin and self-centredness and their hearts have ached. Then God the Holy Spirit has illuminated Christ in all his gracious love. They have felt the drawing power of the cross where Jesus died to take our sins away even while we were enemies of God. They have heard the voice of God in the gospel calling them to trust themselves wholly to Jesus and to live to serve him, and they have responded to that call. That is what constitutes a Christian.

A call always interrupts our usual routine. In the context of this letter, it is worth reminding ourselves that no one can be called by the holy God and continue uninterrupted in the immoral ways of this world.

Loved by God

A Christian, secondly, is someone who is **'loved by God the Father'** (v. 1). 'Doesn't God love everyone?' someone may ask. Yes he does. But for those outside of Christ his love is mixed with sadness and anger. He has a sad, yearning love for the unsaved, as a father might have over a lost child. He has an anger over their sin, as a father might have over a renegade son or daughter who has rejected him, misused his love and refuses to have anything to do with the family. That is the kind of love God has for the non-Christian. But for the Christian God has nothing but love. It is unmixed. The Christian is truly the child reconciled to God as his Father and held in his embrace. God's love for the non-Christian is the broken love of a broken family. God's love for the Christian is the vibrant love of a family in harmony.

Not only is the love that God has for his people an unmixed love, it is also a sovereign love. The conundrum of the relationship between God's detailed predestination of all things and human freedom of choice is not a puzzle which it is possible for us finite creatures to solve. God and his ways are greater than we can ever understand. All we know is that Scripture tells us that when someone becomes a Christian it is because God chose that person, and loved him or her unconditionally before the beginning of time, and in his love infallibly draws the person to faith in Christ. Alongside that, all we know from Scripture is that when people are lost it is because of sin for which they themselves are responsible. It is God's sovereign love *alone* which makes the difference, and rescues us from sin and immorality. The old saying, 'There but for the grace of God go I,' has a very deep resonance in the Christian's heart. It is almost traumatically humbling as we come to realize that only God's love makes the difference.

Kept by Christ

Thirdly, the Christian is someone who is **'kept by Jesus Christ'**
(v. 1). The idea of keeping is something of a theme in Jude's
letter. It comes in verses 1, 6 (twice), 13 (where it is translated
'reserved'), 21 and 24. Once someone is truly reconciled to
God, he will not let that person go. He will keep him or her.

God's agent for keeping his people is his Son, the Lord
Jesus Christ. Keeping is particularly a function linked to the
Lord Jesus. As the book of Hebrews reminds us, his humanity
makes him especially fitted to understand and sympathize with
those who are facing trials and temptations because he has
faced them himself during his earthly life. Furthermore, Hebrews reminds us that the risen and ascended Christ now appears in the Father's presence to intercede on our behalf. We
are reminded of the apostle Peter on the night of Christ's be-
trayal, when Satan wished to sift him as wheat so that he would
deny his Lord, but Jesus said that he had prayed for Peter, and
so Peter would turn back to Christ (Luke 22:31-32). In heaven,
the Lord Jesus performs a similar function for all true Christians even now.

In particular when the churches are flooded with false teaching and immorality, tempting God's children to walk out on
him and his truth, Christ will keep them. Christ will keep a
firm hold on his true people. Putting things another way, the
true Christian is not just someone who makes a decision for
Christ, but someone who sticks with that decision for the rest
of his or her life and goes on with Christ and keeps going to
the end. The Christian *perseveres* in the faith, and Christ *keeps*
us in the faith. These are two sides of the same coin.

The example of Abraham

The call of God, the love of God, and the keeping power of
God — these are the things which constitute a Christian.

We have already alluded to Abraham, the first patriarch of God's Old Testament people, the Jews. In Scripture he is thought of as the father of those who believe. There is a sense in which Abraham's story is a pattern which is replicated in the life of every child of God. When we considered the genealogy of Jesus we remembered that Abraham was an idolater (Josh. 24:2). But in the midst of his worship of false gods, the true God *called* Abraham to leave his old life and follow him. God made him wonderful promises that he would make Abraham into a great nation and give his descendants the land of Canaan. No explanation is ever given as to why Abraham was given such promises and others were not. The answer lies not in any deserving in Abraham, but in the fact that he was sovereignly *loved* by God. Abraham responded to God's call and travelled to the land God had promised. There were many troubles which came upon Abraham, many of them of his own making. Yet each time God stepped in to preserve Abraham. Having turned from idols to the true God, he was *kept* by God through all the long years until he was finally gathered into the glory of heaven. The tale of Abraham is the story of all God's people. In this way we can all, as it were, read our own life in the Scriptures and we praise God for that. We are all called, loved and kept by our God.

Christian experience

Jude now gives a salutation to his readers. It is an embryonic prayer, a wish for the Lord to bless them. As a consequence of what God has done and is doing for us, the Christian experiences, and grows in the experience of, three things. Jude greets his readers with the words: **'Mercy, peace and love be yours in abundance'** (v. 2).

This form of address is interesting. The first two components, 'mercy and peace', were a well-known Jewish form of greeting of the times. The addition of not just 'love' *(agape)*, but 'love in abundance' is more specifically Christian. Together, these components of the greeting are a fairly unusual combination which in a minor way underlines the fact that Jude, our writer, is indeed from a Jewish-Christian background. The three elements of Jude's salutation tell us much about basic Christian experience. These things are to 'be yours'; they are to be the present possession of the Christian.

Mercy

A Christian is someone who knows the mercy of God. A Christian is a sinner. Even after coming to Christ we are still sinners. Every day we deserve God's wrath. But every day God is pleased to be merciful to us through the Lord Jesus Christ. Every day he forgives us. Every day he orders our lives in ways which are beneficial to us spiritually. Every day we have mercies to thank God for. 'He is better to the worst of us than the best of us deserve,' says an old Scots proverb. We feel this in our hearts.

Peace

A Christian is someone who knows the peace of God. As we read Jude, we come across those who will suffer the wrath of God. Jude speaks of 'the punishment of eternal fire' (v. 7) to be suffered by false teachers who live immoral lives. But the Christian is not someone with whom God is at war, but someone with whom God is at peace. The peace treaty between God and the believing sinner has been signed in Christ's blood shed on Calvary. That state of peace is translated into our experience by God's Holy Spirit in our hearts.

Further, in outworking of our Christian lives we experience that peace through faith in Jesus Christ. There may be troubles and trials in our personal lives, or the church itself may be assailed in various ways. Certainly the situation which Jude addresses is one in which the integrity of the church was under attack. Such trials may cause Christians great anguish. But there is a peace of God which passes understanding, which we can know as we commit our ways to him and trust his promises.

Love

A Christian is someone who knows the love of God. In Jude's letter the love of God is that which sustains the Christian in joy and service as we wait for Christ's return. The Christians are told to 'Keep yourselves in God's love as you wait' (v. 21). The word Jude uses for 'love' is the Greek term *agape*. It is a term which particularly applies to the love of God. It is a love which is unconditional and even embraces the unlovely and the undeserving. We experience this love of God through the truth of the gospel and the Holy Spirit's witness in our hearts. It is the knowledge and certainty of the love of God which motivates us and provides strength for us to love others in the way God has loved us. The apostle Paul speaks of the love of Christ constraining and compelling him to persevere in his evangelistic ministry (2 Cor. 5:14). As we know the love of God we find ourselves continually renewed spiritually and a genuine love for others and concern to serve them welling up within our hearts. Love is the great mark of genuine Christianity. Whereas the false teachers are basically self-serving (vv. 16,18), Jude wants to see such unconditional Christian love overflowing in the lives of his readers.

Here we see the pastoral heart of Jude. Every Christian pastor longs to see his people enjoying a well-rounded and close walk with God. The errors of false teaching only ever lead to spiritual disaster.

Jude's greeting indicates something of the dynamic movement of God's grace from heaven to earth. Christians are to
know mercy coming from God, peace in their hearts and love
overflowing in their lives out towards others. It is a wonder-
fully balanced and beautiful Christian greeting.

Conversion

It is the experience of the mercy, peace and love of God through
the gospel which both breaks the heart of the sinner and heals
the soul of the saint. We are sinners by nature, who have broken the divine law and by right should suffer divine wrath. But
it is not the apprehension of that alone which makes a Christian. Rather what makes a Christian is that, knowing our just
condemnation, feeling our sins, we are given a wonderful sight
of the free forgiveness and mercy of God through Christ. Having understood in our souls something of the mighty oncom-
ing storm of wrath we deserve to suffer, we taste the profound
peace that is there for the asking in Christ. Having felt the pain
of God's just rejection of us because of our inbred corrupt
nature, we know the unspeakable joy of being enfolded in the
love of God as the Holy Spirit's presence penetrates to the
depths of our hearts and consciences.

The story is well known but it bears repeating. In 1739 the
great evangelist George Whitefield took to preaching in the
open air. Quite early on he preached to a crowd of degraded
coal miners on the outskirts of Bristol. In a few days he had a
congregation of a few thousand. These men came under conviction of sin and were touched by the mercy and love of God
in Christ.

Whitefield wrote in his *Journal*, 'The first discovery of their
being affected was to see the white gutters made by their tears
which plentifully fell down their black cheeks... Hundreds and

hundreds of them were soon brought under deep convictions, which, as the event proved, happily ended in a sound and thorough conversion.'

What makes the sinner cry? Yes, there are tears of deep sorrow over sin. But those bitter tears are mixed with tears of love as we understand and receive the unparalleled love of God for us. It is a difficult experience to explain to others, but it is perhaps best conveyed when Whitefield and other revival preachers spoke of their hearers being 'melted' under the message of the gospel. The mercy, peace and love of God melt our hearts when we first turn to Christ. This ongoing experience of 'mercy, peace and love' is that which continues to sustain a Christian inwardly through whatever trials and testings he or she may face and motivates the Christian to gladly pursue a practical, healthy and loving Christian walk.

This is true Christian experience. It makes a person very different from the arrogance and boastfulness (vv. 8,12,16), which seem to have been a mark of the false teachers.

What is a Christian? Christians are those who have responded to the call of God, come into the love of God as their Father and keep on in the faith through the keeping power of Christ. Are you a Christian? Are these things realities in your life?

Why is it worthwhile to be a Christian? It is worthwhile to be a Christian because, in a world that is justly bound for hell, we have received mercy through Christ. It is worthwhile being a Christian because in a world in rebellion against God, we are at peace with God. It is worthwhile being a Christian because this world is passing away, but through the love of God we are guided safely into eternal life. Sin can never satisfy. It only leads to destruction. But the Christian has the love of God now and the joy of heaven to come.

Fallen men and women would rather hear other messages. They would rather hear about some method of positive thinking

which promises great wealth. They would rather hear about
how to attain an altered state of consciousness or see an angel.
But what good is great wealth or manufactured excitement in
the face of the fact that one day death will sweep us away and
we must stand before God in judgement? Perhaps they would
rather hear some message about how to have all sickness healed
and enjoy perfect health in this life. But what good is perfect
health in this life if we miss out on heaven in the next? No, true
power lies in the despised gospel of sins forgiven and eternal
life through Christ. This gospel, and this gospel alone, hands
to us the keys to eternity.

2.
Contend for the faith

Please read Jude 3-4

In today's post-modern world, truth is at a discount. Amid our computerized, audio-visual 'information technology' society, people can feel overwhelmed with facts and opinions coming at them from all directions. Doctors have even recently proposed that there is such a thing as 'information overload syndrome' producing chronic stress in people in managerial positions. There is just too much information to cope with.

As our world progresses scientifically, more and more options become available. As our culture becomes more and more pluralist, with the idea becoming accepted that there are many different outlooks on life which are equally valid, there are less and less agreed certainties by which to guide public debate. As our world is increasingly crowded and more interconnected, there are more voices to be heard. For all these reasons and more, many issues in today's society are increasingly complicated. Some of us may feel they have become impossibly complex.

Against such a background some people are tempted to give up on reason as a guide to life. Thinking things through has become far too difficult. Instead they opt to be guided by feelings and images. The most important question for them about something is no longer 'Is it true?' but 'Do I like it?' or 'Does something feel good or look attractive?' The answers to these questions are far more simple to resolve. The whole of rock-music culture and consumer society projects the approach which tells people that life is about how you feel. Even if people do try to answer questions rationally, things are so complicated that they have lost confidence in being able to decide the right answer. It is so much easier, it is said, to just go along with your feelings. Life becomes a game of chance in which you risk all on your intuition. Young people see it as adding excitement to life. Rationality is boring. So truth is left to one side.

In such a world, unwary Christians can be influenced along similar lines. Christian faith based on the Bible seems too unexciting, and they are tempted to leave the old paths of **'the faith that was once for all entrusted to the saints'**, to follow preachers who claim continual extraordinary spiritual experiences and dispense feelings of ecstasy through their fingertips. Increasingly, even in the church, emotions are everything, while truth is out of fashion. Obviously there is nothing wrong with emotion. We do need to feel our faith. But if the pursuit of emotion is given priority over the use of our minds, labelling careful thought as unspiritual, then the church is facing certain disaster. We must **'contend for the faith'**.

Among Christians there is another factor at work as well. In an age that has given up on truth the church can bend over backwards to be seen as loving and caring. In doing this it shies away from making a stand for the truth. The motives may be laudable, but by this route a dangerous indulgence has crept into the church which is alien to the real spirit of the New Testament. Referring to the incident in 1 Samuel 15 where King Saul neglected to obey God's command to destroy all the Amalekites, A. W. Tozer puts it like this: 'The fashion now is to tolerate anything lest we gain the reputation of being intolerant. The tender-minded saints cannot bear to see Agag slain, so they choose rather to sacrifice the health of the Church for years to come by sparing error and evil; and this they do in the name of Christian love.'

But according to Jesus the truth matters, and could not matter more. We are saved through gospel truth. We are given eternal salvation as we receive the truth of Christ into our hearts.

Jesus said, 'If you hold to my teaching, you are really my disciples. Then you will know the truth, and the truth will set you free' (John 8:31-32). Paul spelled out that to be saved is to 'come to a knowledge of the truth' (1 Tim. 2:4). Note that there is, according to both Christ and his apostle, such a thing as 'the truth'. What we like is no sure guide to salvation. It is through the truth that people are saved. Truth is vital.

The thrust of the letter

It should not surprise us, then, that Jude is concerned for the truth. In these verses he gives us something of a synopsis; he sets out the theme of his letter in a nutshell: **'Dear friends, although I was very eager to write to you about the salvation we share, I felt I had to write and urge you to contend for the faith that was once for all entrusted to the saints'** (vv. 3-4).

Jude was not someone who relished controversy. Rather, he relished the gospel and rejoiced in its encouragements. He liked being positive rather than negative. He would have much preferred to write a letter of rejoicing in the glories of Christ and the privileges which Christians share. But sometimes we have to postpone what we would like in order to do what is needed. Sometimes Christians have to risk being labelled intolerant and to fight for the truth. As Jude writes, this was such a time. The church was under threat from persuasive immoral heretics. It was no good shirking responsibility. Jude felt compelled to stand up and be counted for the cause of Christ.

His letter comes as a clarion call to our generation as well. A lethargic strategy always commends itself to fallen human beings. We can all feel that it is easier to keep our heads down and hope for the best. But wars are never won like that. Jude would shake us out of complacency and urge us to take a stand along with him.

The faith we promote

Certain things in the Bible are not so significant as others. For example, Christians argue and can afford to disagree over what the Scriptures teach about the way to organize the government of the churches. Baptists disagree somewhat with, say, Presbyterians, or Anglicans. These things are not vital to salvation. In the early church Christians had differences of opinion on eating meat bought in the market which may have been offered as a sacrifice to a pagan idol. Romans 14-15 tells us that such matters are matters of conscience and each individual Christian must act according to his conscience and let others do the same in such matters.

But there are other matters which are absolutely vital for salvation. Not to believe them is to be lost. For example, the apostle John insists on Jesus' full deity as the Son of God (1 John 4:15), and cites the doctrine of the full humanity of the Lord Jesus Christ (1 John 4:2-3). Not to trust in Christ, God's Son, as one who, apart from sin, is in every way human as we are, is no small matter. Rather, John declares, those who deny this and propagate such ideas are caught up in the spirit of antichrist (1 John 4:3). They are not God's children. They are lost.

At the beginning of 1 Corinthians 15, the apostle Paul underlines some of the matters which he sees as of 'first importance' to the Christian faith: 'Christ died for our sins according to the Scriptures ... he was buried ... he was raised on the third day according to the Scriptures' (1 Cor. 15:3-4). Note the emphasis on Scripture, human sin, and on the cross and resurrection being understood in the context of atonement for sin. To reject Christ's atoning death and his bodily resurrection from the dead is to 'have believed in vain' (1 Cor. 15:2). Not to hold firmly to these things is not to be a Christian.

So to tamper with the gospel, or to teach a different gospel, is a heinous crime in the view of the New Testament apostles. Paul, in his letter to the Galatians, could not be more strident: 'But even if we or an angel from heaven should preach a gospel other than the one we preached to you, let him be eternally condemned! As I have already said, so now I say again: If anybody is preaching to you a gospel other than what you accepted, let him be eternally condemned!' (Gal. 1:8-9).

In our verses Jude underlines two things about this precious gospel.

1. It is complete in its truth

We are called to **'contend for the faith that was once for all entrusted to the saints'**. God's truth has, of course, been revealed over many centuries. There has been a process of revelation. Old Testament history reaches back a long way. We think of Abraham, to whom God spoke. We come on a few hundred years to Moses, through whom God gave the first five books of the Bible. After the nation of Israel had settled in the land King David wrote the Psalms. A number of centuries later we come to the time of the great writing prophets like Isaiah and, later, Jeremiah. Later still, after the exile in

Babylon, but still some 400 years before Christ, the prophet Malachi wrote the final book of the Old Testament. The book of Hebrews sums up this process of Old Testament revelation by saying, 'In the past God spoke to our forefathers through the prophets at many times and in various ways' (Heb. 1:1).

Yet that unfolding revelation of God's truth came to completion in the time of the Lord Jesus and his apostles. Jesus is none other than the Word of God incarnate (John 1:1,14). No fuller revelation is possible this side of glory. God spoke in Old Testament times, says the writer of Hebrews, 'but in these last days he has spoken to us by his Son'. Matthew 1:23 tells us that Jesus is 'God with us'. The Lord Jesus was able to say to his disciples, 'Anyone who has seen me has seen the Father' (John 14:9). So it is that, with the coming of Christ and the giving of the New Testament, revelation of God's truth for salvation is complete. There is no more to be added, for there is nothing more to be added.

Jude underlines that for us when he tells us to 'contend for the faith that was *once for all* entrusted to the saints' (v. 3).

If the truth is all there in Scripture, then we must be alert to all those religious people who try to add to it. The Mormons are false teachers, for they tell us that we not only need the Bible but must supplement it with Joseph Smith's *Book of Mormon*. The Jehovah's Witnesses are false teachers, for they tell us that we can only understand the Bible as we read it alongside the literature produced by their organization in New York. Traditional Roman Catholicism is false teaching, for it would compel us to put the traditions of their church and the pronouncements of the pope alongside the Scriptures.

There is a proper place for true charismatic gifting in the church. However, the Word of God is complete and cannot be added to in any way, whether by the preacher or by any form of so-called 'prophet'. Many who claim to be gifted men and women today have taken a false path. We do not claim that there are no instances in which God appears to have given special insight to an individual, such as, for example, the well-known story of C. H. Spurgeon while preaching at the Surrey Gardens Music Hall. He suddenly pointed to a man in the crowd he did not know and said, 'There is a man sitting there, who is a shoemaker; he keeps his shop open on Sundays, it was open last Sabbath morning; he took nine pence and there was fourpence profit out of it; his soul is sold to Satan for fourpence!' It turned out to be all true and was the means by which the man was led to conversion. Spurgeon goes on to say that he could tell of a dozen cases in which similar things happened.[1]

However, whenever a modern 'prophet', either explicitly or implicitly, gives the impression that what he or she is saying is new truth, or is to be taken and acted upon as if it had the authority of Scripture, binding people's consciences to respond, then such people have become false prophets. The truth of Scripture has been once for all given to the church, and by the truth of Scripture all else is to be tested.

This is such a fundamental issue that it is worthwhile spending time underlining this matter from other passages of the New Testament. This idea that the Christian revelation is complete is not an idea peculiar to Jude.

In the upper room on the night he was betrayed, after Judas had departed, Jesus spoke to his faithful disciples about the coming of the Holy Spirit. We are given a detailed account of what he told them there in the Gospel of John. Throughout chapters 14 to 17, Jesus repeatedly designates the Holy Spirit as 'the Spirit of truth', for one of the Spirit's main tasks is to superintend the communication of truth.

To those eleven apostles in that upper room Jesus said, 'But the Counsellor, the Holy Spirit, whom the Father will send in my name, will teach you all things and will remind you of everything I have said to you' (John 14:26). Notice that

Jesus promised, not that the apostles would be taught 'some' things, but that they would be taught *all* things by the Spirit — all things pertaining to God's salvation. The faith given through the apostles in our New Testament is complete. How was John able to write such a detailed record of what Jesus said to them in the upper room? Precisely because the Spirit fulfilled Jesus' promise that he would 'remind you of *everything* I have said to you'. There is no more new revelation and there is no secret teaching of Jesus we need to know hidden in the sands of an archaeological dig, or in some as yet undiscovered 'Gospel' locked away in the vaults of a museum. The faith has been *once for all* given to the church.

Later in the same upper room discourse, Jesus went on to tell his disciples, 'But when he, the Spirit of truth comes, he will guide you into all truth. He will not speak on his own; he will speak only what he hears, and tell you what is yet to come' (John 16:13). We notice again that Jesus promises that his apostles will be led into *all* truth. This truth pertains not just to their own time, for they were shown 'what is yet to come'.

We should not be surprised, therefore, that this completeness of the truth of the Christian faith is spelled out practically in the rest of the New Testament.

What does Paul write concerning those who would teach a different gospel? 'I urge you, brothers, to watch out for those who cause divisions and put obstacles in your way that are contrary to *the teaching you have learned*. Keep away from them. For such people are not serving our Lord Christ, but their own appetites' (Rom. 16:17-18).

What does Paul say concerning the qualifications required in those who would be church leaders? 'He must hold firmly to the trustworthy message *as it has been taught*, so that he can encourage others by sound doctrine and refute those who oppose it' (Titus 1:9). The true church leader continues to teach what has always been taught without changing it, because the faith we contend for is a completed body of truth.

There are to be no additions to, and no subtractions from, Scripture. All that we meet with in our Christian experience is to be tested by the Scriptures. This stance is absolutely crucial to the health of the church. It has always been a battleground down all the ages of church history and will continue to be so, especially in coming years. The Christian doctrines of revelation and of the authority of Scripture are issues on which every Christian, especially those in positions of leadership, needs to have the matter well thought out and to be crystal clear.

2. *It is entrusted to the church*

Jude tells us to 'contend for the faith that was once for all entrusted to the saints'. The word **'saints'** means 'holy ones', but in the New Testament it does not refer to special holy people, or people who have performed particularly heroic deeds in the service of God. It is simply the New Testament word which is used to refer to all Christians. We are all holy people as we have been cleansed from our sins and set apart for God in Christ. Together, Christian people, 'the saints', make up the church.

The gospel is not a message invented by the church or by its preachers. It is a message which comes from God, but which has been placed into the hands of the church.

Heavenly truth has been **'entrusted to the saints'** (plural). It is the work of the church together to guard and look after the truth of the gospel. Down the ages that work has gone on. Apostles have preached and taught it. Ordinary Christians shared it with neighbours and lived it out in their lives. Before the days of printing some people spent all their lives in the work of copying the Scriptures, faithfully writing out each word, so that today the Bible is, without parallel, the best-attested book of ancient times. Linguists have laboured to accurately translate the Scriptures into the common languages of the world. Theologians dedicated themselves to express as clearly as possible Bible truth and its implications systematically in the creeds of the church. Martyrs have given their lives at the stake rather than deny one iota of the truth of the Christian faith.

Times do change. Culture moves on. Jude and the other apostles lived before the days of high technology communications and modern urban society. Therefore the church's task is an ongoing one. The church must do its best to express the truth of the gospel in language which is appropriate to the times and which contemporary people can understand. But its task in this area is simply a task of accurate rendering, not of rewriting the gospel story and gospel truth. We are called to be interpreters, not authors.

When a political leader goes to another country for important discussions with people who speak a different language, he or she will take an interpreter along. The politician has important things to say which he does not wish to be misunderstood. The interpreter's job is definitely not to change the meaning of what his leader wants to say, but simply to translate it as accurately and as faithfully as possible into the foreign tongue. In just the same way, the church is called to be Christ's faithful interpreter to its contemporary world. We must work at producing accurate Bible translations readily understandable to people. Preachers must work diligently at making the gospel clear and readily accessible, but also at handing on the truth as we find it in the Bible uncorrupted. Our task is at all costs to preserve the truth of the gospel, while at the same time making it understandable to our peers who are alienated from, and foreigners to, the things of God.

The body of Christian truth which Jude calls **'the faith'** is the treasure of God given to the church. It is the church's great treasure because by it people are saved and taken from the abject poverty of sin and given the riches of eternal life in Christ. So it is that the church has sought to defend the faith and contend for the faith. Paul wrote to Timothy, 'What you heard from me, keep as the pattern of sound teaching, with faith and love in Christ Jesus. Guard the good deposit that was entrusted to you — guard it with the help of the Holy Spirit who lives in us' (2 Tim. 1:13-14).

Not only are we to defend the truth against false teachers. The word **'contend'** here implies that, but it implies much more as well. We must go on the offensive. We must positively spread the true gospel. Jude's call to contend for the faith is therefore also a call to evangelism and apologetics. Preachers are to preach the Word. Individual Christians are to witness for Christ. By our lives we are to commend the gospel. By our support we are to encourage missionary endeavours. By our prayers we are to battle in the heavenly realms for the advance of the 'faith that was once for all delivered to the saints'.

But the battle to contend for the faith is not simply a struggle for doctrinal purity or evangelistic potency. As the rest of the epistle of Jude makes clear, it is a struggle to maintain a godly lifestyle within the church, as the lifestyle which ought to be the resulting fruit of the gospel in people's lives. The separation between belief and behaviour flows from ideas of the Enlightenment, not from the Bible. The idea of knowing the truth but not living it is anathema to biblical thought. It would mean that actually a person does not *know* the truth at all. In verse 4 Jude speaks of false teachers who make the grace of God into a licence for immorality. It is not only against devious teaching, but against sinful behaviour among professing Christians that he calls us to battle when he calls us to 'contend for the faith'. Belief and behaviour are always linked. To contend for the faith means concerning ourselves with Christian duty as well as Christian doctrine.

We must contend for the faith whether the gospel is popular or whether it is not. We must do this when society believes in God and when it does not. We must do this when it is intellectually respectable to be a Bible believer, and when it is not. We must do it when the established church hierarchy are good men committed to the truth, and when they are heretical liberals who sneer at the old gospel. We must do it when Christianity is the dominant faith in a country, and when it has to jostle in the religious market-place of a pluralistic society. The church must do this whether it is in the midst of a rising civilization or whether its culture is collapsing all around it. The church must do it in a modern world of science and objectivity, and in a post-modern/New Age world dominated by image and subjectivity. The church must do it when it is in the midst of heaven-sent revival, or when it is suffering, dwindling and small. The church's primary call is not be to popular among people, but to be faithful to God. The call to battle is clear: 'Contend for the faith.'

The opposition we face

This call, then, is always applicable. But why in particular does Jude feel he has to stir up the church to contend for the gospel? He tells us: **'For certain men whose condemnation was written about long ago have secretly slipped in among you. They are godless men, who change the grace of our God into a licence for immorality and deny Jesus Christ our only Sovereign and Lord'** (v. 4).

The church was being corrupted by false teaching and false teachers. If the truth is lost or perverted then the devil will have halted or hindered the work of salvation. In order to contend it is vital, therefore, that both Jude's readers and we ourselves should be able to recognize false teachers. Jude tells us four things about them to aid us and encourage us.

1. Their predictable condemnation

First, he seeks to encourage us. We are not to lose heart in the face of rampant false teaching. Jude tells us, concerning false teachers, that **'Their condemnation was written about long ago.'** Where was it written about? Jude has the Scriptures in mind. Later in his letter, in verse 11, he is going to cite three examples of false teachers of previous generations who troubled God's people. But throughout Old Testament history people arose to oppose God's true servants. Elijah was opposed by the prophets of Baal (1 Kings 18). Micaiah was opposed by the false prophet Zedekiah (1 Kings 22:11,24-25). Jeremiah was opposed by the false prophet Hananiah (Jer. 28). The Lord Jesus himself was opposed by the majority of the religious establishment of his day. The devil is real and there has never been a time when he has not raised up people to stand against the truth of God one way or another.

'So do not be surprised that you have to contend against false teachers,' Jude is telling us. We are not to be frightened, or perplexed, or disappointed, that we have to battle with heresy. We may say to ourselves, 'Wouldn't it be nice if all the church was one, and everything was sweetness and light among those who profess the name of Jesus?' We may understandably yearn for such a time when there will be no trouble in the church. But we are living in dreamland if we think that such a time is ever going to arrive this side of glory. We are just not facing spiritual reality. We are in a battle, and shall be until Christ comes.

But the combination of warning and encouragement that Jude gives us is that such false teachers will not finally succeed and they will get what is coming to them.

Not only, by implication, has their presence among us been predicted, but their *condemnation* has been foretold as well. Read the Old Testament stories. See, for example, the end to which the prophets of Baal came (1 Kings 18:40). Read, as another example, what happened to the false prophet Hananiah, who tried to oppose Jeremiah, God's true messenger (Jer. 28:15-17). Specifically, in verses 5-7, Jude will go on to remind us of Old Testament incidents which spell out the truth that those who rebel against God face a coming judgement of the severest kind. He will also later in his letter use the 'prophecy' of Enoch and the warnings of the apostles to drive home the same point (vv. 14-19). They are bound for destruction. Their destiny has been writ large for a long time. So do not be frightened or dismayed by them. Certainly do not be tempted to follow them. Rather, do your duty and contend for the faith.

2. Their subtle methods

No false teacher arrives in the church with a placard around his or her neck saying, 'I am a false teacher.' They do not announce their treachery against Christ. Many of them, having been deceived themselves, are not aware of their own error and therefore are very sincere in their belief that they are saying and doing the right thing (2 Tim. 3:13).

Whether consciously or unconsciously, false teachers always come in disguise. Jesus told us all that 'They come to you in sheep's clothing, but inwardly they are ferocious wolves' (Matt. 7:15). As God's vulnerable flock we need to be alive to the subtle methods and disguises of such wolves. Often false teachers are immensely plausible. Jude says the false teachers have **'secretly slipped in among you'** (v. 4). There is a stealth and underhandedness. They have insinuated their way into the congregations.

Their *teaching* often seems very plausible. All the 'best' and most destructive heresies are made up of half the truth.

That is why the church can be taken in. These half-truths are usually mixed with ideas which particularly appeal to our fallen nature. They flatter us, or they spell out what seems to be an easier path which leads to heaven.

Their *persons* often seem very plausible too. They can be extremely charming people in their dress and demeanour. Often they are very affable and able to make a congregation relax with their humour. Frequently they are highly educated, perhaps sporting a string of degrees with letters after their names. Sometimes they are even able to perform what appear to be supernatural signs and miracles. Jesus said, 'Many will say to me on that day, "Lord, Lord, did we not prophesy in your name, and in your name drive out demons and perform many miracles?" Then I will tell them plainly, "I never knew you. Away from me you evildoers"' (Matt. 7:22-23). There is nothing wrong, *per se,* with being a charming, witty person, or being well educated, or necessarily anything wrong with supernatural happenings (if they are real). But the point is that none of these things is a proper test of whether or not someone is true or false as a teacher.

We must not be diverted. We must keep our eyes on the crucial questions: 'Is this person's teaching completely scriptural? Does he live a godly life?' We must be clear what tests we must apply.

3. Their immoral lifestyle

Jude goes on to describe the false teachers who are threatening the churches of his time saying, **'They are godless men, who change the grace of our God into a licence for immorality'** (v. 4).

The devil's purpose behind the false teaching is always somehow to legitimize sin. He wants the church to be duped into thinking that morality does not matter: 'What we are doing is not wrong.' There will be no more confession and repentance.

There will be no more looking to the blood of Christ for cleansing. This will defile the church and ruin its relationship with God and its witness to the world. Church history is, of course, littered with examples of just this.

For example, some of the so-called 'radicals', during the time of the English revolution of the seventeenth century, preached total sexual permissiveness. One, Abiezer Coppe, misusing Christ's command to become as little children said, 'And to such a little child, undressing is as good as dressing ... he knows no evil.' Another famous example is the Russian monk Rasputin, who insinuated his way into the circles of the Russian tsar at the beginning of the twentieth century perpetrating immorality. He belonged to a group called the Khlysty, who believed, to put it bluntly, that the more gross the sin, the deeper would be the shame and so the more real the repentance. God would forgive. The idea was that sin brought spiritual good.

But one does not have to look at the annals of history to find the tendency to change the grace of God into an excuse for sin. Paul recognizes in his letter to the Romans that some people were already seeking to misuse the grace of God in this way. Having spelled out in detail the glories of God's free grace, he pre-empts the question of his opponents when he writes, 'Shall we go on sinning, so that grace may increase?' (Rom. 6:1). His resounding answer is, of course, 'By no means!' All such attempts to teach that the gospel means that sin does not matter do not come from God. To be a Christian is to be joined spiritually to Christ, who is holy. How, then, can we possibly go on in sin, or try to legitimize it?

Today not a little of the radical church is being influenced by post-modernism and New Age ideas. As we have already noticed, these approaches to life speak in terms of cutting loose from the traditional understanding of truth and shaping one's own reality. Morality is just another part of that malleable

world. Imagination is reality and all things are possible. With
such an outlook you can easily justify calling evil good and
good evil.

Even sections of the contemporary evangelical church which
seek be faithful to the Scriptures also face attempts to turn the
grace of God into a reason to embrace sin within the church.
'Does God not love adulterers, or thieves, or homosexuals, or
alcoholics?' we are asked. The implication is that if God loves
them, then we should accept people as they are within the fold
of the church. But this is to pervert the truth of the love of
God. Yes, God loves all sinners, and every true Christian is
still a sinner. But part of becoming a true Christian is to sincerely own Jesus as Lord and seek with God's help to obey
him. This means that, whatever our besetting sins, we must be
seeking to fight against those sins in our lives, not trying to
legitimize them or say they do not matter.

It is false teachers promoting the acceptance of immoral
sexual practices whom Jude has particularly in mind as he
writes. But let us remember there are others. The love of money
is seen as just as spiritually defiling as sexual immorality in the
New Testament (Heb. 13:4-5). 'God wants you to be rich,'
some tell us. 'God wants us to have a good time,' they preach.
But this attitude promotes the perspective of this world, not
the perspective of eternity. Such a worldly viewpoint is the
mark of false teachers (1 John 4:5). The true Holy Spirit is the
life of heaven and of the world to come. When he comes into
a person's life, that person's viewpoint is changed. The false
teacher is marked by worldly ways.

4. Their heretical doctrine

Jude tells us, fourthly, that the false teachers **'deny Jesus
Christ our only Sovereign and Lord'** (v. 4). Classically heretics have more often than not held erroneous ideas about the

person of the Lord Jesus Christ. The Jehovah's Witnesses deny the full deity of Christ, seeing him merely as the highest creation of God. The Mormons accept that Jesus is the Son of God, but ultimately only in the sense that any human being can be viewed as a child of God. The old liberal wing of the church denied the bodily resurrection of Christ, which the New Testament sees as the great declaration that he truly is the Son of God and Lord of all (Rom. 1:4).

Many ordinary Christians have had the impression that the so-called 'Faith Movement' is basically an orthodox evangelical group with just an off-beam idea about health and wealth. Sadly this is far from the case. Behind the error which promotes 'faith' as a Christian version of the power of positive thinking, lurks a totally false view of God himself. One of the American prosperity teachers has actually said that there are nine persons in the Trinity. Another has said that God told him that, if he had enough faith, he could have done the work of dying for the sins of the world just as well as the Lord Jesus.[2] False teachers come with heretical doctrine.

The heretics whom Jude is opposing were marked by denying Jesus Christ as our only Master and Lord. Some commentators have argued that this denial of Christ was not a doctrinal matter, but simply another way of articulating the fact that they were disobedient to the Lord's commands to live godly lives. Though immoral behaviour is a denial of the Lord, this is unlikely to be the case. I say this, first, because generally moral aberrations are justified by some kind of doctrinal foundation and, secondly, because the internal evidence of the epistle indicates otherwise.

The internal evidence within the letter needs to be noticed at this point.

Firstly, if the Christology of the heretics was impeccable then their deviation could be expressed simply in terms of denying Jesus as Lord. But Jude, in verse 4, tells us that there is a pluralism about their ideas. They deny him as 'our *only* Sovereign and Lord'.

Secondly, Jude has chosen a very unusual word to assign to Christ. He says that the false teachers deny Jesus Christ as our only *despotes* (Sovereign or Master). As we have noted previously, this is a word only used of Christ here (v. 4), and in the parallel epistle of 2 Peter. The use of this peculiar term in and of itself seems to imply that the false teachers did have a deviant view of the Lord Jesus Christ.

Perhaps, by way of explanation, it is worth noting that the phrase 'deny Jesus Christ our only Sovereign and Lord' is parallel to an expression in *The Book of Enoch* 48:10 which says, 'They denied the Lord of Spirits and his Messiah.' Some scholars argue that Jude has modelled his words in verse 4 on this quotation. If this is true, then the phrase seems to be especially linked to the idea of lordship over angelic beings.

Further, we are told later in the letter that their attitude is to 'reject authority' (v. 8). They were a law unto themselves. This must imply a false view of the Lord Jesus Christ. In fact some commentators argue that the words in verse 8 should be translated, 'reject the authority of the Lord'. This, taken with their lordly 'slander [of] celestial beings', indicates that these false teachers probably saw themselves as on a par with Christ. He was not the only lord. They too were lords. This sort of outlook emerges when people pursue a theology which denies the pre-existent deity of Christ and sees Jesus as simply the first true Christian, the first to receive the grace of God.

More evidence for such a view of the false teachers' understanding of Christ comes from Jude's failure to use any direct teaching of Jesus in his letter, or to refer to Jesus by way of example. The only New Testament teaching Jude uses is that of the apostles with whom his readers have had direct contact and through whom they had their first experience of God's grace. Evidently his first point of entry in using this teaching is his readers' personal experience, rather than the authority of their Lord. Similarly, in dealing with the false teachers' slandering of celestial beings, it would surely have been of use to refer to the examples of casting out demons in the Gospels, or the way the Lord Jesus handled Satan during his temptation in the wilderness, or his contacts with angels, as in Gethsemane and elsewhere. The fact that such incidents are passed over would indicate that the example of Jesus did not cut any ice with the false teachers. This would make sense if they saw themselves as lords as well. Though it is an argument from silence, it seems significant.

Two lessons

There are two great lessons which we need to fasten on to as we leave these vital verses.

The first, naturally, is the need to be both *guarding* and *promoting* the biblical gospel. This calls for spiritual maturity in every aspect of our personalities. It calls for a sharp and biblically informed mind, for heresies are often very subtle. It requires a firm will, a courageous resolve, for we shall meet much opposition as we try to stand for the truth. It also requires a loving heart, because to pursue the inevitable controversy involved in defending the faith in a way which delights in scoring points over others is ugly and spiritually disastrous. The gladness with which we declare the free love of God in the gospel must be matched by the sadness at having to oppose others who deny it.

Every Christian has a responsibility to do what he or she can to contend for the faith. But the elders, evangelists and pastors of the churches are those who particularly are charged with this responsibility. This has practical consequences for us. As we bear in mind the spiritual qualities required to do this work well it should prompt us to pray for those who lead our churches. Pray that God will equip them in mind and will and heart. Also, as leaders do take a biblical stand in the midst of controversy, we have a responsibility to get behind them and give faithful men support, by encouraging and standing with them.

The second lesson which suggests itself very powerfully from these verses is the need for the church to maintain the doctrine of Christian conversion. At root the false teaching which insinuates that immorality of various kinds is acceptable within Christ's church is telling us that people do not have to be changed to be saved. But that is not true. How can someone be truly born again and yet continue living the same kind of life as before? It is impossible.

Although it is true that, through Christ in the gospel, God accepts us just as we are, yet he does not leave us like that. He begins a new life in us. God's Holy Spirit takes up residence in our hearts and begins the ongoing transformation of our lives. In the current world which fosters a live-and-let-live culture, and looks upon all kinds of perversities as equally acceptable lifestyles, it is essential that the church clearly maintains the doctrine of new birth and Christian conversion. Especially when churches are small and we long for growth, it is easy to let this slip in our eagerness to gain new members.

1. *Spurgeon: The Early Years,* Banner of Truth, 1967, pp.531-2.
2. See Hank Hanegraaf, *Christianity in Crisis,* Harvest House Publishers, USA.

3.
The judgement of God

Please read Jude 5-7

Memory is a most important faculty for any human being. Without it we should not be able to learn anything. Without it how could we follow any logical argument? Without it how could we even find our way home? The call to remember is especially vital in our times. We live in days in which TV fun-culture encourages us to focus almost exclusively on the here and now. We are the children of an era which sees 'progress' as good and the past as obsolete. Such an atmosphere stifles inner reflection and breeds social and historical amnesia.

The Bible is full of calls for us to remember. The nations who forget God go down to the grave (Ps. 9:17). We are called to remember the Lord and all the way he has led us (Deut. 8:2). We are to remember the Sabbath day (Exod. 20:8). In particular, as Christians, we are commanded to remember the Lord and the Lord's death at the communion table, until he comes (1 Cor. 11:23-26).

These verses of Jude's epistle are in a similar vein of remembrance: **'Though you already know all this, I want to remind you that the Lord…'** (v. 5). Jude recognizes that his readers are already well aware of the basic Bible stories to which he is going to refer. In one sense he is only going to tell them what they already know. But though they know the biblical narratives, Jude is concerned that they have forgotten the true significance of these stories. It is not simply the facts they need to grasp, but the meaning. The Old Testament stories are not simply fascinating tales of antique interest. The book of Romans states that 'Everything that was written in the past was written to teach us, so that through endurance and the encouragement of the Scriptures we might have hope' (Rom. 15:4). The stories have a moral to them of which we need to take note.

In verses 5-7 Jude gives his first set of three. They are three Old Testament warnings. The point of these stories is to show to us that rebellion against God can never succeed. He reminds his readers about the rebellion of the children of Israel in the wilderness (v. 5), about the rebellion of the angels (v. 6) and about the rebellious lifestyle of the cities of Sodom and Gomorrah (v. 7). Each of these rebellions ended in the judgement of God upon those involved.

Why does Jude want to remind his readers of these gruesome things? It is, of course, because of the situation which his readers face. As we have seen, Jude is writing to Christians at a time when the church is being assailed by false teachings which encourage people to immorality (v. 4). There are false teachers with novel, yet attractive, ideas which in effect draw people to walk out on the biblical gospel. Christ offers us new life which includes both the forgiveness of sins and the call to a holy life. To pursue immorality rather than holiness is a denial of that gospel, even though it may pretend to be done in the name of Jesus. To walk out on the pursuit of holiness is also to walk out on forgiveness. If we thus leave the gospel of the Lord Jesus Christ, we expose ourselves to the judgement of God! So these Old Testament stories could not be more relevant. They underline Jude's reason for writing his letter, which is to warn the church not to follow these licentious heretics.

Often the corrupting message of false teachers comes along under the guise of being some new revelation from God, or the latest spiritual insight which has lain undiscovered for years.

But Jude, the half-brother of the Lord Jesus, has already reminded us that the faith which we defend, and for which we
are to contend, is 'the faith that was once for all entrusted to
the saints' (v. 3). It is complete in its truth. There are no legitimate additions to be made to it, or subtractions to be made
from it. We have seen that the faith of the gospel is the only
medicine which can cure the sickness of sin and its consequences. It is entrusted to the church and must not only be
kept pure, but its instructions followed carefully.

We have also seen that false teachers and heretics are subtle
in their methods (v. 4). They can, on the surface, be very nice
people, very intelligent and presentable people. Some of them
may even be able to perform miracles of a kind. Yet, whether
consciously or unconsciously, their whole direction is to lead
people away from following Christ in humility, faith and holiness. In the hands of Satan, the purpose of false teachers and
false teaching is to give legitimacy to sin in the eyes of people
and so tempt them away from Christ. In the face of such subtlety
Christians need warnings which are sharp and vivid, loud and
clear, to prevent them from being taken in. To walk out on
Christ and follow another 'gospel' is to walk out on salvation
and into damnation. So it is that Jude brings these three striking examples of God's judgement from the Old Testament.
'Whatever you do, don't follow them!' he is urgently shouting
to the church.

Immorality today

Our contemporary church scene reflects that which Jude is
addressing very closely. Since the beginning of the 1960s Western society generally has been on an uninterrupted slide into
decadence and degeneracy. Perhaps the watershed in Britain
came with the court case over the publication by Penguin Books

of *Lady Chatterley's Lover* by D. H. Lawrence. It concluded with permission to publish and all 200,000 copies sold out on the day it appeared. From then on all kinds of material was allowed into the public domain masquerading as art. Along with this, also in the 1960s, the contraceptive pill came onto the market and into society. By the 1970s in Britain the pill was available to single women as part of the National Health Service. The pill offered the prospect of sex without pregnancy and this too accelerated the so-called sexual revolution. This moral slide has, sadly, rubbed off onto the church at large.

Whatever we think of the Established Church, its influence on the nation generally has always outstripped that of other churches. In those early years of the 'permissive society', the intellectuals of the Church of England had imbibed liberal theology which rejected the absolute authority of Scripture and sought to construct a faith which was based more on experience and the fashionable intellectual fads of the time. For example, in 1963 Bishop John Robinson published his book *Honest To God*, which attacked the biblical understanding of the person of God, as outdated in the modern world. Not too long afterwards his radical theology was followed by a loosening of ethics. Cutting loose from the commands of Scripture, he trumpeted the so-called 'situational ethics'. Such people as Robinson taught that Christians should not necessarily be duty-bound to an absolute morality, but should allow themselves to be led by 'loving' feelings and the perceived needs of others. Pre-marital sex could be justified sometimes, it was said. Without the sure anchor of Scripture this soon opened the door to degenerate practices becoming more and more acceptable to the church. Any attempt to question such acceptance of sin was quickly condemned as 'intolerant', 'unloving' and 'bigoted'. Confused and embarrassed and not wishing to be labelled in such a way, the church began to wilt morally. Sadly, it was not too long before things unheard of before in evangelical circles, divorce and sex outside of marriage, began gradually to appear in the churches. Later we have seen the rise of a 'Christian' lobby promoting homosexuality and lesbianism as acceptable in the church. This is the direction from which the current church came to find itself in a position so similar to the one Jude is addressing.

The God of judgement

Before we look further into the text of verses 5-7, we need to realize afresh the main point of these verses. This is that God is a God of judgement. This is not a popular doctrine. It never has been in the past and it is not now. The whole of modern liberal society revolts against the idea that we are responsible sinners, accountable for our actions to a holy God.

The humorist P. J. O'Rourke is only slightly exaggerating when he writes, 'The second item of the liberal creed, after self-righteousness, is unaccountability. Liberals have invented whole college majors — psychology, sociology, women's studies — to prove that nothing is anyone's fault.' We live in a culture where everyone wants to paint him or herself as a victim of circumstances and elicit sympathy from others, but no one wants to own up to being a responsible agent of hurt or evil.

The Bible rejects this attitude as self-deception: 'If we claim to be without sin, we deceive ourselves and the truth is not in us' (1 John 1:8). There may be mitigating circumstances for people's actions, but there are no exonerating circumstances for evil. God is a holy God and will bring all to judgement.

People come back at the Christian teaching with a furious question: 'How can a God of love be a God of judgement?' The implication is that love and judgement are incompatible and if God is not a God of love then they are morally superior to him and he is not worth bothering with anyway. But they are wrong. True love and judgement are perfectly compatible and, indeed, God would not be a God of love unless he were also a God of judgement.

Think of the example of a surgeon who cares deeply about his patient. The patient has a death-dealing cancer. The surgeon, because he cares for the patient, will cut it out and go on to recommend action to destroy every vestige of it with chemotherapy or nuclear medicine.

In the same way, Scripture tells us that God loves his creation, the world he has made, and because he loves it he will judge all evil in it. Because he loves it, as he sees sinners destroying it and destroying the image of God in one another by our evil, he will cut it out; he will send judgement. If people retort that God should be more committed to them personally than to his world as a whole, that simply provides even more proof of how self-centred we are and how inextricably wedded we are naturally to sin. If the idea that God is committed to something bigger than us offends us, what does that say about us?

God will judge, and the whole of the Christian gospel is predicated upon that fact. If there is no judgement Jesus did not need to come and die to save us, for there is nothing to be saved from. But he did come to die, and therefore we must take the warning of a coming judgement day with absolute seriousness. A God of love will send people to hell if they are determined to go on in sin and reject the truth of Christ. And whether we are open atheists, or we disguise our rejection of Christ under a cloak of church attendance, or religiosity of another kind, makes no difference. To be living a life which either overtly or covertly rejects following Christ in the way of holiness is to be outside his forgiveness and so exposed to coming judgement.

'Not everyone who says to me, "Lord, Lord," will enter the kingdom of heaven,' said Jesus, 'but only he who does the will of my Father who is in heaven' (Matt. 7:21). Against the background of the sexual antics of our contemporary world, that saying of Jesus is brought into sharp focus when we lay it alongside the words of the apostle Paul in Thessalonians 4:3-5. What is God's will? 'It is God's will that you should be sanctified: that you should avoid sexual immorality; that each of you should learn to control his own body in a way that is holy and honourable, not in passionate lust like the heathen, who do not know God.' Paul realizes that this may not be immediately attainable by a Christian but often involves a process of learning to control ourselves. We are saved by God's grace, not by our holiness. A true Christian is prepared to learn, with God's help, to be holy. But to embrace some teaching which seeks to legitimize that which the Bible condemns, and continue in practices which God forbids, is to put oneself outside the grace of God, even if what is done is done under a banner which calls Jesus 'Lord'.

With all this in mind, then, Jude reminds his readers in the church of three Old Testament stories of the judgement of God.

The people of Israel (v. 5)

Instead of taking the three stories in chronological sequence, Jude picks out the rebellion of the people of Israel in the wilderness and puts it first. This is probably to draw particular attention to it in a stark way. The reason for this is that the situation of the Israelites is of special significance to professing Christians: **'Though you already know all this, I want to remind you that the Lord delivered his people out of Egypt, but later destroyed those who did not believe.'**

The Exodus is the great Old Testament redemption. God saved his people out of slavery in Egypt and was taking them to Canaan, the land of milk and honey. They had been rescued, but they had not yet arrived in the promised land. Like the people of Israel, we professing Christians live out our lives between two salvation events. We have trusted Christ, who died and rose again, but we are not yet in heaven.

On the way to the promised land, while they were in the wilderness, Israel rebelled against God on many occasions and brought God's judgement upon themselves. Those who were initially rescued from slavery never arrived in the land of promise. The precise occasion of rebellion to which Jude is referring is left open. A number of occasions when the children of Israel rebelled could be in Jude's mind. He particularly mentions unbelief, and many commentators take the line that he is referring to their failure to believe on the borders of the promised land which is recorded for us in Numbers 13-14. Moses sent in the spies, who came back with a report that, although the land was fruitful and beautiful, yet the people who lived there were strong and their cities well defended. The majority of the spies concluded that it would be far too difficult for God's people to enter and take possession of the land. Only Joshua and Caleb, from among the spies, said that with God's help the Israelites could win Canaan for themselves. With the pessimistic majority report uppermost in their minds, the people failed to believe the promises of God and rebelled. Their unbelief brought down God's judgement and he condemned that generation to not entering the promised land, but to wandering for forty years in the wilderness until a new and more trusting generation had arisen. This is a warning to us. 'They were not able to enter, because of their unbelief' (Heb. 3:19). We must believe God, no matter how unlikely, at a human level, his promises may seem. In the context of Jude's epistle, perhaps we could say that a failure really to believe in God's promise of heaven does lay us more open to being tempted by the promises of the fleeting pleasures of sin in this world.

However, perhaps the incident of unbelief on the border of the promised land recorded in Numbers 13-14 is not that which is uppermost in Jude's mind in these verses. Rather, unbelief is

the root of all disobedience and, with the background of verse
4 and its reference to immorality, it may be the occasions of
sexual sin among the children of Israel that are in the forefront
of Jude's thought.

The first great rebellion was the worshipping of the golden
calf, which occurred when Moses was first up on Mount Sinai
receiving the Ten Commandments. Moses' absence for such a
long time was the occasion for them to forget what God had
done for them through Moses. They made themselves an idol
and fell into revelry as they worshipped it. The Hebrew word
translated 'indulge in revelry' in Exodus 32:6, where this incident is recorded, often has sexual connotations. On reaching
the scene, Moses gave his great call, 'Who is on the Lord's
side?' The Levites came to Moses' side and Moses commanded
them to kill those who would not stop. Three thousand of the
people died. Through unbelief those who had escaped from
Egypt were judged for their disobedience.

Of particular relevance, however, is the rebellion which
occurred at a place called Shittim. Under the instigation of the
false prophet Balaam (see Rev. 2:14), to whom Jude will later
refer in verse 11, the Moabites enticed the men of Israel. 'The
men [of Israel] began to indulge in sexual immorality with
Moabite women, who invited them to the sacrifices of their
gods' (Num. 25:1). This may have especial bearing on the
church in Jude's mind for two reasons.

The first is because the word he uses for 'immorality' in
verse 4, in a Jewish context, would connote not only its basic
meaning of irreverence and unrighteous conduct, but would
point particularly in the direction of sexual sins. If Jude is particularly concerned about sexual immorality in church circles
then this rebellion is of especial note.

The second is that this immorality at Shittim took place in
the context of religious worship of the Baal of Peor. Baal is a
word meaning 'Lord'. In that sense, it took place in the name

of the 'Lord'. Sometimes things can go on in churches 'in the name of the Lord' which are actually sinful and blasphemous. God's response to this rebellion by his people was to send a plague against Israel which was only halted when those who had given themselves to this immoral worship were put to death (Num. 25:5,9).

Professing Christians are in a parallel situation. We live between having come to Christ and having reached heaven. The cross has rescued us from sin and we are en route to our eternal promised land, but we have not yet entered. If we are faithful and stay with Christ throughout our lives it will show that we are true Christians. If we are faithful and follow Christ to the end, we are absolutely safe and shall certainly enter the glories and joys of heaven. But if we rebel and follow other 'gospels' peddled by ungodly false teachers, we shall prove that our profession of faith has never been properly rooted in Christ. If we walk out on Christ and being a godly Christian disciple we too, like the rebellious people of Israel, shall come under judgement and never reach the promised land.

The central lesson here is the necessity of ongoing faith in Christ and in God's Word. God **'later destroyed those who did not believe'** (v. 5). Faith is crucial. We must, with God's help, determine to keep on believing and so obeying Christ every day. We need to think about that practically.

We live in a culture which is saturated with atheism and agnosticism. The press, TV and other media are dominated by these ideas. The prevalent lifestyle of our Western world is materialism. It is only visible, touchable commodities which truly matter, we are told. Our faith is forever being challenged: 'You can't really believe that old gospel from that old Bible!' Yet, without being obscurantists, we have got to determine to believe Christ, and follow him intelligently, every day.

The devil not only brings pressure to bear on us intellectually; he also brings pressure to bear on us morally. 'Walk out on Christ,' whispers Satan. 'Sin is far more fun than being a stuffy Christian.' Or, 'Go along to a church which is less demanding morally; you will be OK,' he says. 'God understands: you can have your habitual peccadilloes, and still be a Christian.' Yet, without becoming legalists, we have got to determine to keep believing, to take up the cross, deny ourselves and follow Christ every day.

But if we do fall into sin we must keep believing then too. For when we stumble while seeking to follow Christ, the devil will come to us again, but with a different story. He will then say, 'It is no use. You have fallen again. God is finished with you. There is no forgiveness now. You may as well close the door behind you on Christian faith.' Yet we must keep believing. We must ignore Satan's insinuations and believe what Scripture says — that God is ever merciful to all who come to him. We may feel, like the prodigal son, that we have sinned so much and brought God's name into such disrepute that we are no longer worthy to call him our Father. Yet, like the prodigal son, we must return and, as we do, we shall find that God's love knows no bounds for us. We must keep believing the gospel. The good news of forgiveness is not just for the unsaved. It is for Christians as well!

We must keep believing and so go on following Christ.

The angels of heaven (v. 6)

For his second example of God's judgement Jude directs our attention to the invisible, spiritual world of the angelic beings. Jude refers to the angels often in this short letter and this may reflect the Jewish background of the letter; the Jews of the first century seemed to show much interest in apocalyptic visions and the angelic world.

Jude explains: **'And the angels who did not keep their positions of authority but abandoned their own home —**

these he has kept in darkness, bound with everlasting chains for judgement on the great Day.'

Once again the reference is ambiguous. These verses could refer to the original fall of the angels in following Satan in rebellion against God. But, with the high probability that Jude particularly has in mind the idea of sexual immorality in the churches, and this as an expression of ungodliness and rebellion against God's commands, it seems that he is more likely to be referring to the strange occurrences recorded for us in Genesis 6:1-4.

Angels, according to Jewish tradition, left heaven to marry and have sexual intercourse with human females and so increased the corruption of the human race in the period before the Flood. This story features prominently in *The Book of Enoch* from which Jude later quotes in verses 14-15. According to the commentator Richard Bauckham, 'This was how the account of the "sons of God" in Genesis 6:1-4 was universally understood (so far as our evidence goes) until the mid-second century A.D. ... though the tradition took varying forms. From the time of R. Simeon b. Yohai in the mid-second century A.D., the traditional exegesis was replaced in Judaism by an insistence that the "sons of God" were not angels but men. In Christianity, however, the traditional exegesis had a longer life, questioned only in the third century and disappearing in the fifth century.'

If this is the incident, and the general understanding of the incident, to which Jude is referring, then the scenario would be as follows. These angels had some God-given position of authority and were very blessed by God. But, not satisfied with the role God had given them, they crossed the boundaries God had set by intermarriage and sexual relations with human beings.

Whether Jude has in mind the original angelic fall or this understanding of Genesis 6 is not crucial to our understanding. Either way, the angels rebelled against their God-given position,

disobeying the command of God. The consequence was that
they brought down the judgement of God upon themselves:
**'These he has kept in darkness, bound with everlasting
chains for judgement on the great Day.'** It is worth noting
Jude's wordplay here. These angels did not *keep* their God-
appointed positions, so now they are *kept* to face judgement.
The wordplay emphasizes the appropriateness and justice of
God's judgement and at the same time warns us to *keep* to
Christ ourselves.

Jude speaks of the angels being bound with 'everlasting
chains', to await judgement. The *Book of Enoch* uses this precise language, but also Isaiah's prophecy speaks similarly in
reference to heavenly powers:

> In that day the LORD will punish
>   the powers in the heavens above
>   and the kings on the earth below.
> They will be herded together
>   like prisoners bound in a dungeon;
> they will be shut up in prison
>   and be punished after many days
>
> (Isa. 24:21-22).

The mention of 'everlasting chains' is meant to warn us that,
without true repentance, momentary sinful rebellion can have
eternal consequences.

This reference to angels being judged may seem rather eso-
teric to us on first consideration. Why does Jude choose to set
before us an example concerning angels? 'I am not an angel,'
we may be thinking to ourselves. 'What has this got to do
with me?'

The answer is to be seen along these lines. The angels are
very exalted beings. Some people who are very gifted and
very blessed by God can fall into thinking that somehow they

are above the regulations which apply to other people. This seems, as I have previously argued, to be parallel to the attitude of the false teachers whom Jude was opposing. They may not say so outright, but there is an unconscious assumption that 'I am so blessed by God, so necessary to God's plans, so useful to God, that I am beyond having to worry about God's law. I have special treatment from God. I am above having to obey like other people.' Jude's point is that if the angels are not above having to obey God's commands, then neither are you! Whoever you are, whatever your spiritual abilities or intellectual powers, never think that God's law does not apply to you!

Never listen to false teaching which speaks of some spiritual blessing which puts you on a different plane from 'ordinary Christians'. Never think that you can reach a level at which obedience to Scripture does not matter to you. Sadly, there are many ideas around today which tend in this direction. There are many churches in which the Bible and obedience to its commands are downplayed or neglected in place of other things. Perhaps it is the slogan that we are 'not under law but under grace' which is bandied around, misunderstanding what the apostle meant when he used that phrase. Perhaps it is that priority is given to supposed contemporary revelations of the Spirit which lead people along this line. But nothing which is truly of the Spirit will lead us into disobedience to the plain commands of Scripture. The Bible was inspired by the Spirit and the Holy Spirit does not have a forked tongue. Whatever it is, we must reject anything which encourages us to in effect put ourselves above Scripture.

We have a most sad illustration of this very situation in the Old Testament. We remember the amazing gift of wisdom given to young King Solomon when he first came to the throne of Israel. Because, when God came to him in a vision, he asked for wisdom to govern God's people well, the Lord was pleased with him and granted him great wealth and power as well. But in his old age we read that the wise Solomon became a fool. He took foreign wives who worshipped foreign gods, something the books of Moses warned against, and he wandered away from the Lord and brought trouble upon his people. At the end we are not even sure that Solomon was saved. Only eternity will tell. We are to take heed of such an example. No matter how influential, rich, powerful and wise we may be, we should never think we have leave to follow after disobedience to God.

This is particularly relevant to us in our post-modern society. Our contemporary world is moving increasingly towards the idea that all morality is relative. Ethical behaviour is seen as all a matter of culture. Different people have different opinions as to what is right. Different cultures have different ideas about rules for living. 'So,' our peers conclude, 'morality is all of human making. We know better than previous generations. We are sophisticated. We will choose our own morality.' And the implication is: 'If the morality which we make for ourselves happens to be that which was viewed as immorality in other times and cultures, so what? It doesn't matter.' We have in effect placed ourselves above morality.

By his story of the angels Jude is warning us that it is not true. God's law stands. It stands above the world, above time and above all earthly cultures. It even applies to the angelic beings. Why? Because God's law is the expression of the holy character of the Lord which is eternal and does not change. If God judged the angels who ignored his command, do not be so foolish as to think that morality is relative and changeable. Do not be taken in by such teaching, no matter from what source you hear it. Do not be taken in by it whether it comes from the lips of an urbane Oxbridge academic, a charismatic prophet, or an enthusiastic preacher with a Bible in his hand.

The cities of sin (v. 7)

'In a similar way, Sodom and Gomorrah and the surrounding towns gave themselves up to sexual immorality and perversion. They serve as an example of those who suffer the punishment of eternal fire.'

Advocates of the 'gay' lobby within the church have been heard to argue that the sexual sins of Sodom and Gomorrah were not the central reason why God judged the cities. Rather, they say, it was more for their lack of concern for the poor and needy that God destroyed them (Ezek. 16:46,49-50). But this is an unnecessary cavil. Both lack of compassion and sexual perversion are detestable to God. The two sins go hand in hand in a materialistic society. Here, in Jude, we are told quite plainly that sexual immorality and perversion were the reason for God's judgement. This ought to be enough for the modern church to take heed and be warned about seeking to legitimize such practices under the name of Christ. Let us say again, we are all sinners in various ways and Christians, more than anyone, should be ready to acknowledge that. In Christ there is forgiveness for sinners. But whatever our besetting sins, be it homosexual practice or anything else, the Christian's life must be about seeking to overcome them, not to legitimize them.

The cities of Sodom and Gomorrah were in a beautiful position on a plain. The book of Genesis tells us, 'The whole plain ... was well watered, like the garden of the LORD, like the land of Egypt, towards Zoar' (Gen. 13:10). But that did not lead the people there to be grateful to God their Creator. Rather, like our prosperous society of today, they became arrogant, overfed and unconcerned, and fell into detestable ways. We sometimes are given the impression that secularism is a phenomenon which has taken Christianity by surprise as it has swept across the world with the rise of affluence generated by the technological revolution of the past few hundred years. This is a fallacy. The Bible clearly spells out, again and again, that when people become prosperous they have a propensity to forget God. As one wit has commented, 'He who sets out to serve both God and Mammon very soon realizes that God does not exist.' God warned his people of this in the book of Deuteronomy as they were about to enter Canaan (Deut. 8:17-18). The writer of the book of Proverbs pleaded with God that he should not become rich, 'Otherwise, I may have too much and disown you and say, "Who is the LORD?"' (Prov. 30:9). And where God is forgotten, human beings are wide open to believing they can think and behave as they please with impunity. Here in the people of Sodom and Gomorrah we meet a regular feature of fallen human nature.

Jude highlights the sexual immorality and perversion of these cities. We are given some insight into this by the Genesis story of the angels sent by God, following Abraham's intercession, to save Lot and his family who were living there: 'All the men from every part of the city of Sodom — both young and old — surrounded the house. They called to Lot, "Where are the men who came to you tonight? Bring them out to us so that we can have sex with them"' (Gen. 19: 4-5).

The misuse of God's gift of sex here is not simply that it is of the nature of casual gratification outside a committed relationship. The problem rather is that God's gift of sex is meant to be used only within the committed relationship of marriage between male and female. This is how God intended sexual relations to be, as is witnessed by the record in Genesis chapter 2, with the creation of Adam and Eve. The one-flesh relationship is to be between a man and wife. Because God ordered things this way at creation, 'For this reason a man will leave his father and mother and be united to his wife, and they will become one flesh' (Gen. 2:24). Thus homosexual acts are condemned throughout the Scriptures (Lev. 18:22; 1 Cor. 6:9-10). They were not part of the original creation which God pronounced 'very good'. Homosexuality is a 'perversion' (v. 7). It brings down the judgement of God upon people. Do not be deceived. It brings down the judgement of God, even upon those in the professing church.

Likewise, the stories of angels seeking sexual relations with women, from Genesis 6, would be a breach of God's created order and equally to be condemned. The men of Sodom pursued homosexual activity. Probably they were unaware of the heavenly origin of Lot's visitors. Here too we have the possibility of sexual relations between humans and celestial beings. We can only wonder as to why Jude has chosen to select two examples which involve angelic/human relations. Perhaps it is purely 'accidental', but if our thesis is correct that the false teachers saw themselves as in some way superhuman, lords of angels, and they were pursuing immoral liaisons with people within the churches, Jude's choice of these examples would have had significance to his original readers.

There are a number of plain lessons which we must not pass by here.

1. We are told that the destruction of these two cities of sin serves as **'an example of those who suffer the punishment of eternal fire'** (v. 7). We must take the faithful warning that there is an eternal fire for all who abuse God's gifts and refuse to repent and seek forgiveness and transformation in Christ. There are many pictures of the nature of hell; here it is set forth as a fire. Here too, as elsewhere in the Scriptures, we are warned that the duration of hell is for ever; it is 'eternal' fire (cf. Matt. 25:46). In a sermon entitled 'Everlasting Oxidisation', C. H. Spurgeon addressed the question of how something could burn for ever and not be totally consumed. Surely, the burning must lead to an eventual annihilation? His answer,

as he sought to be faithful to Scripture, was to point his hearers to the material we call asbestos, which is able to be put in a fire, but never consumed.

2. Such teachings give us no pleasure to repeat, but we are to take the warning and flee from unholiness. We are not saved *by* our holiness. We are saved by the wonderful free grace of God. But we are saved *for* holiness, and if holiness is not our aim, and if we fail to make strides towards holiness, then these are marks that we are not saved. The plain statement of the New Testament is this: 'Make every effort to live in peace with all men and to be holy; without holiness no one will see the Lord... See that no one is sexually immoral' (Heb. 12:14-16). Someone may object, 'I thought that once I was a Christian, Christ would keep me safe to heaven! So why does God's Word have to contain such notices of danger?' The answer is that Christ does keep his people. But one of the ways he uses to keep us is through giving us warnings, and the chief sign that we are his people is that we take his Word and his warnings seriously. The Lord Jesus is the Friend of sinners. He will forgive and never turn away any who come to him. But we must come to him sincerely, not only willing to be forgiven, but willing to seek to be obedient to his commands.

Immorality and TV culture

In concluding this chapter it is worth reflecting a little more deeply on the question of the temptations concerning immorality. Again, let me stress that we are all tempted in many different ways, and in considering this particular matter we are not seeking to condemn people who struggle in this particular matter more than others. But God's Word teaches that if we reject his norms of behaviour, built into the world at creation, we shall wreck our lives and the lives of others (Rom. 1:24,27).

The hold which sexual immorality has on our Western society is shown especially by our use of the TV media. A report from the US in 1998 said that pornographic video sales and rentals had increased 100% since 1992. Pornography at the end of the century is a \$4.2 billion industry in America. The information came from the industry's trade magazine *Adult Video News*. It means that in the US pornography is a business twice as big as baseball and three times bigger than Disney's theme parks. These figures do not include internet pornography, which is booming. In Britain figures in 1998 showed that most visits to internet sites were for pornography.

Another symptom of our culture's decadence is the way the homosexual question is being thrust ever more prominently onto the agenda of the church. One of the main arguments that Bible-believing Christians run up against in this controversy is the idea that if homosexual practices take place between two consenting adults, then it does no one else any harm and so is no one else's business. The implication is that people should just be left alone.

But, firstly, it is highly questionable that homosexuality is a private matter in this way with no public consequences. The promotion of homosexual practice does undermine the biblical view of family life and we are already seeing vast consequences of this in the unhappy society we are creating. Not only so, but the gay lobby presses ever more boldly for the lawful age of consent which defines 'consenting adults' to be lowered and, in response to this pressure, in Britain Parliament has recently voted to make such acts legal at sixteen years old. The assumption is that homosexuality is something inborn, so this will not affect those who are not already gay. But the Bible tells us that all sinners are corruptible. People who are not homosexual in outlook can be led into it.

Secondly, the argument that homosexual practices produce no visible harm is highly dubious. Medical evidence, which is often suppressed by our media, shows that in fact there are fearful consequences for those who are committed to a lifestyle of sexual immorality. The use of condoms has failed to make sex 'safe'. The most disturbing evidence of the health dangers run by those who indulge in homosexual practice was seen in some research published in 1994. The authors analysed 6,500 obituaries from the gay press in the USA and compared them with obituaries from conventional newspapers. Whereas the median age of death for ordinary married men was seventy-five years, for the homosexual deaths the median age was thirty-nine if death was AIDS-related and forty-two if from causes unrelated to AIDS.[1]

Then, perhaps more importantly, even apart from the overt pornography industry, we need to realize that we are a culture dominated by TV and this medium is often used to promote sexual immorality generally. In the very way it relates to us as human beings we need to realize that TV can be a deceiver.

TV drama series and films often broadcast scenes of sexual immorality. The focus of these scenes is the temporary sensual pleasure of the illicit affair. These are thrust to the forefront before the viewer. But in real life, sexual immorality frequently leads to feelings of guilt and worthlessness afterwards. This is hardly ever referred to on TV. In real life, adultery often breaks up families, with children being seriously damaged psychologically. This is rarely shown. In real life an immoral lifestyle frequently spreads many kinds of destructive diseases and side-effects. These are not often mentioned. The list could go on. More often than not, the TV is a liar concerning sexual activity. Yet it holds such a powerful sway over people's thinking and behaviour. As Christians, under the pressure to forget from the TV culture, Jude calls us to remember what God has said.

Further, the TV tells us lies in another way too. The 1960s media guru Marshall Mcluhan produced a famous adage. He said, 'The medium is the message.' What he meant was that the *way* a message is communicated to us is a message in itself. One of the hidden messages of TV has to do with the fact that our ability to see is an instantaneous faculty. We can only see what is now. Jude tells us that memory is a crucial faculty (v. 5). We mentioned at the beginning of this chapter that because TV concentrates on the faculty of sight it brings with it the subtle message that 'Now is the only time that really matters.' It tends to disengage us from the past and the future. As Bible-believing Christians, though we do realize the importance of grasping the moment, we have to reject the idea that life is to be lived only with an eye on the present. If nothing matters but now, that provides a total justification for sensual and immoral living. It tells us not to think about consequences, but if we feel like it, just do it. Such an outlook implicitly and totally rejects biblical morality. Though now is important, we cannot understand it aright without looking both at the past and the future. In the past we have been made by God to whom we are accountable (vv. 5-7). In the future we are led to see there is an eternal judgement (v. 7). To cut the present away from the past and the future is disastrous for a true outlook on life. Again we see that, especially in the area of sexuality, the TV is often a vehicle of untruth.

Naturally, the idea of the judgement of God is something we would rather forget than remember. The TV age, with its continual focus on the here and now, encourages us to put 'the day of the Lord' out of our minds. But we are fools if we do. Jude therefore stirs up our memories. We need to be reminded.

1. P. Cameron et al, *The Journal of Death and Dying,* 1994, 29, 249-271

4.
Not all false teachers are the same

Please read Jude 8-13

I was brought up in the 1950s and when I was a youngster it was the fad for little children to be given regular doses of cod liver oil. This tasted absolutely foul but it was meant to aid your development, protect you physically and make you strong. Perhaps some parts of the Word of God are like that; they do you good but they taste bitter sometimes. Parts of the Bible are more difficult, more unpalatable than others. This section is in some respects a distasteful section. But God has put it in the Scriptures for our benefit. We must not leave out the difficulties of the Bible. Very often the best jewels are in the deepest, darkest mines and the Lord Jesus has put these difficult parts of Scripture there for our learning.

You will see, if you cast your eyes over verses 8-19, that there is a repeated phrase. It is the phrase **'these men'**. In verse 8, we read of 'these dreamers', and then in verse 10 the same persons are referred to: 'Yet these men speak abusively.' Again in verse 12 we read, 'These men are blemishes at your love feasts,' and then in verse 16, 'These men are grumblers.' In verse 19 Jude writes, 'These are the men who divide you.' Of course, 'these men' who are being referred to are the false teachers who have crept into the church. We are only going to proceed to verse 13 in this chapter because there would be too much material to cover in one chapter. But the whole section hangs together.

'These men', then, are the false teachers who have slipped into the churches during Jude's day and who are causing havoc by teaching very wrong things about the Lord Jesus Christ and the grace of God. Because of their error, ungodly behaviour and immorality threaten the churches. Jude writes to thwart 'these men'. The actual Greek word he uses is *houtoi*, which is just the masculine form of 'these' and usually means 'these men'. Its repetition could be construed as quite scathing.

If the scenario which was sketched out in the introduction has any truth to it, then the false teachers probably saw themselves as special beings, on a par with angels, if not above them in status. They put around the idea that somehow they were superhuman. No doubt they would have used such ideas to bolster their status within the churches and perhaps to help seduce their victims into committing immorality with them. Jude's concern by the repetition of the phrase 'these' would be to contradict this claim. They are not extra-spiritual beings. They are merely common men.

In the previous chapter we saw that Jude's first priority was to warn the churches. He writes to warn the Christians not to follow these people who are perverting the gospel and encouraging ungodly living and immorality. 'Don't follow them,' he has said, 'because they are leading you to destruction.' To adopt a settled lifestyle of immorality is to walk out on Christ. 'If you actually walk out on Christ and follow them, this will be rebellion against Christ and will bring down God's judgement,' he has warned them.

The very same way

In the last chapter we saw three examples of God's judgement in verses 5-7. At the beginning of our present section Jude continues to underline to us that false teachers are following the same path that brought down God's judgement on those particular characters that he has already mentioned. In verse 8 he says, **'In the very same way...'** (the same way, you see, as the children of Israel, the cities of the plain and those rebellious angels — in the very same way), **'... these dreamers pollute their own bodies, reject authority and slander celestial beings.'** This is a rerun of things that have happened before. Christians are not to be taken in by the same old trap. So he is warning, 'Keep away from these things. When you come across false teaching and ungodliness, identify it and get away from it. Never follow it, no matter how tempting it seems.' That is the continuing thrust, as we come to verses 8-13.

The false teachers are marked by three things: polluting their bodies, rejecting authority and slandering celestial beings (v. 8).

Polluting their bodies

Sexual immorality is seen by Scripture as spiritual pollution. Paul reminded the Corinthians that their bodies were temples of the Holy Spirit and therefore not to be defiled by sexual immorality (1 Cor. 6:19). If we take the reference to unbelieving Israel in verse 5 to be alluding to the sin with the golden calf, and understand the reference to the fallen angels in verse 6 to allude to possible angelic relations with human females in Genesis 6, then all three examples of judgement which Jude has quoted in verses 5-7 followed some form of sexual immorality. 'These men are following the same road, and it ends in the same place,' Jude is warning his hearers.

Rejecting authority

False teachers generally reject the authority of others. They sweep aside any idea of coming under the discipline of local churches and their leaders. They see themselves as above such things, ignoring the authority of soundly appointed elders. If the local leaders are faithful men, seeking to adhere to and apply the Scriptures, then actually they are rejecting the authority of the Word of God, and indeed of the Lord himself. **'Rejecting authority'** (v. 8) can be translated, 'rejecting the authority of the Lord'. It may be that the particular false teachers whom Jude is confronting saw the Lord Jesus as just one master who had understood some of God's truth and saw themselves as being on a par with him. Such people would have no problem in setting aside the authority of Jesus in the light of their own revelations.

Slandering celestial beings

Thirdly, Jude sees the false teachers as slandering celestial beings. From the immediate context of verse 9 it would seem that Jude understands the term **'celestial beings'** used here to include evil spirits. Some commentators scorn the idea that Jude is on the side of being 'polite to the devil'. Yet, it is worth bearing in mind that the New Testament teaches that Christians are to show deference to all those in civil authority in this world and to treat them with respect (e.g., Rom. 13:6-7; 1 Peter 2:13-17). This is to be done even in times of persecution. If we are to be polite to worldly authorities, even wicked ones, it seems entirely in line with New Testament spirituality not to be involved in slandering angelic authorities. Godly people are marked by godly language whoever they may be addressing. Scripture calls us not to let any unwholesome talk come out of our mouths (Eph. 4:29).

It is worth adding that this idea of slandering angelic beings is unique to the false teaching combated in Jude and 2 Peter (cf. 2 Peter 2:10). This fact indicates that Jude is confronting a specific and actual case of false teaching, rather than just false teaching generally.

Jude's use of extra-biblical quotations

But before we get further into the text, there are some problems that challenge us in this passage to which we need to refer first. In this passage, as we have previously noted in the introduction, Jude chooses to quote episodes from extra-biblical material. He quotes things about Moses which are not actually in the Bible. Later on we shall see, in verses 14 and 15, that he tells us some things that Enoch is supposed to have prophesied that are not specifically in the Bible and, on the surface, we may find that very disturbing. I can remember as a young Christian first coming across these things and being very thrown by them: 'Does that mean that Jude thinks that these strange books that he is quoting from ought to be in the Bible? Have we got our canon of Scripture wrong? Why does he use these passages and not Scripture?' All these kinds of funny queries come up, don't they? Well, the answer is, no, Jude did not believe these strange books should be in the Bible. But let me just point out three things.

Extra-biblical sources are quoted by other biblical writers

The first thing is that there is nothing unusual about biblical writers referring to literature which is not in our Bibles. Let me give you some examples.

It is worth looking at Numbers 21:14. Moses is speaking there about something of the wars of Israel and he says, 'That is why the Book of the Wars of the LORD says...' and then he gives a quotation. Well, the Book of the Wars of the LORD is not in our Bible, but Moses quotes from it.

We can also pick out a couple of New Testament examples. In Acts 20 Paul is giving his farewell discourse to the Ephesian elders and he is encouraging them to be generous and benevolent and kind to those who need supporting financially. He wants to encourage the elders to do the same. He says in verse 35, 'In everything I did, I showed you that by this kind of hard work, we must help the weak, remembering the words the Lord Jesus himself said: "It is more blessed to give than to receive."' Now, you can look through the Gospels and there is nowhere where the Lord Jesus actually said those words, and Paul appears to be quoting what was well known but not actually recorded in the Gospels.

We find Paul doing something similar in Acts 17:28. Speaking on the Mars Hill in Athens to the philosophers, this time he quotes a Greek poet. He says this: '"For in him [that is, in the Lord, in God] we live and move and have our being." As some of your own poets have said, "We are his offspring."' Paul is using the words of a pagan poet to illustrate his point.

So other books, other sources, are sometimes quoted in the Bible. This may be for a number of different reasons.

It may, of course, be because there are true things which are recorded in other books which are not in the Bible. We could quote from a mathematics book, for example, and it may tell us something that is actually true. It is not in the Bible but it is true, and therefore if, for some reason, a biblical writer wanted to refer it, he could bring that in because it is the truth. The Christian is never to be afraid of anything that is true. God is the God of all truth.

On the other hand, sometimes, a biblical writer may want to quote from other sources for other reasons. It is likely, for example, that when Paul repeatedly uses the phrase, 'Everything is permissible for me,' in 1 Corinthians, he is quoting from the teaching of those he is opposing, in order to address their arguments. He does not agree with their teaching, but he is quoting from it. So biblical writers may quote from sources outside Scripture, and they may do so for different reasons.

The nature of the works quoted

The second area to be aware of is the nature of the two books from which Jude quotes. The *Assumption of Moses* and the *Book of Enoch* seem to have been well known in certain Jewish circles during the early Christian centuries. People converted out of Judaism would have been familiar with them. However, it is possible to get hold of versions of these books today from academic libraries. Besides being enormously preoccupied with celestial beings, we find that they have a very different tone and message from even the more apocalyptic books of Scripture, like Daniel and Revelation. There is little sign of the grace and mercy of God in these books. They appear to focus on the works of individuals as the source of their righteousness, rather than God's love and salvation as a gift. This being the case, it seems unlikely that Jude is quoting from these books because he fully approves of them. We may quote from a well-known hymn, or from *Pilgrim's Progress*, in a sermon, because parts of them may encapsulate the scriptural point we are trying to make. They are not the Bible, but we fully approve of them because they are scriptural. Jude's use of these inter-testamental books is unlikely to be in this vein. He is a Christian who delights in God's mercy, love and grace (vv. 2,4). He exhorts his readers to wait for God's mercy, to keep themselves in the love of God, and show mercy themselves (vv. 21-22). With these gospel notes so clearly missing from *The Book of Enoch* and *The Assumption of Moses*, it seems most unlikely that Jude views these books as full of truth and total allies of Christian faith.

The false teachers would have made use of these sources

So then, thirdly, it seems much more reasonable to see Jude's quotations from these books in terms of his quoting from sources which the false teachers would have made use of in trying to further their claims. These strange books were familiar to the Jewish hearers. If our reading of the nature of the heretics' teaching outlined in the introduction is near the mark, then they were claiming for themselves experiences similar to those associated with this inter-testamental literature. *The Assumption of Moses* purports to give a revelation of the history of the Jews addressed to Joshua, Moses' successor. *The Book of Enoch* depicts Enoch as travelling in the spiritual realm and having conversations with angels. The false teachers were using these supposed revelations and journeyings in the spirit to bolster their corrupt teaching. 'These kinds of experiences happen,' they would have said. 'Look at the experiences of Enoch from these books which you know so well. Look at how the writer of *The Assumption of Moses* witnessed the angelic confrontation between Michael and Satan. Similar experiences have happened to us. Hidden truth has been revealed to us.'

But Jude, it seems, sees here an opportunity to strike back at the heretics on their own ground, for whereas they are purveying immorality on the basis of their angelic revelations, *The Book of Enoch* and *The Assumption of Moses* stand for righteousness. They may do so rather legalistically, but nevertheless they do so. 'How can they claim to follow in the footsteps of Enoch, or in the footsteps of the writer of *The Assumption of Moses*, when they are peddling immorality and rejection of authority?' Jude is asking. He thus uses this material to show that the case made by the false teachers does not hold together. His use of these quotations is akin to Paul's quoting the catch-phrase of the false teachers in 1 Corinthians. He does not have to approve of these books to use them in his argument.

This then, it seems, is a fair way of understanding Jude's use of this literature. It makes sense and at the same time does not in any way impugn the canon of Scripture.

Now, in verses 9-13, Jude gives us three warnings about false teachers. We shall see in verses 9-10 that he tells us about the ignorance of false teachers. Then in verse 11, we are going to be shown different types of false teachers because they are not all the same. Later, in verses 12-13, Jude exposes the effects of false teachers.

The ignorance of the false teachers (vv. 9-10)

First, we look at verses 9-10, where we are told of the ignorance of false teachers. They come to us saying, or at least implying, that they are very wise. They flaunt their own authority and give the impression that they know so much more than we do. With the pretension to revelatory dreams (v. 8) and to having walked among angels, this would certainly have been the air of the false teachers. But Jude is saying that actually they are ignorant. In fact, in verse 10 he says many of them are no different from animals in their motivations.

Here in verse 9, we have yet another of Jude's threesomes. It is the trio of Michael, Moses and the devil who are referred to from the inter-testamental literature. This is a difficult story to understand but the central thrust is clear. These false teachers are arrogant, rebellious and abusive; if these people were really spiritual, they would not have the attitudes that they have, or use the language they do. **'In the very same way, these dreamers pollute their own bodies, reject authority and slander celestial beings. But even the archangel Michael, when he was disputing with the devil about the body of Moses, did not dare to bring a slanderous accusation against him, but said, "The Lord rebuke you!"'**

We will consider the details of the story in a moment, but the main point is clear. It has to do with authority. The false teachers are those who 'reject authority'. This legitimizes their polluting their bodies with immorality and expresses itself in their slandering celestial beings (v. 8). Their idea of experiencing the full grace of God was to be lifted to a status where we are freed from all authority and obligation. This shows itself too in the doctrinal aberration of denying Jesus Christ as our only Sovereign and Lord (v. 4). But here Jude is showing that such an idea was never held by godly people, not even the writer of *The Assumption of Moses*. Here Jude mentions not just angels but the archangel Michael. There is an authority structure even among the angels. He goes on to quote how even the archangel answered Satan, not in terms of his own authority, but said, 'The Lord rebuke you.' Even the archangel acknowledges the authority of the Lord. And of course, having used the title 'Lord' for Jesus Christ in verse 4, it is plain whom Jude regards as the Lord. The conclusion is that the radical rejection of authority, even the authority of Christ, perpetrated by the false teachers finds no foundation in this inter-testamental literature.

Having located the main point of the quotation, let us now look at the detail. This is a strange scenario. What is Jude talking about? As we have seen, he is referring to a story, probably from the lost ending to *The Assumption of Moses*. There are two approaches to understanding the story here.

The older Bible scholars think that what is being referred to here is the idea that God buried Moses' body in a secret place. When we come to the end of Moses' life in Deuteronomy 34:5-6 we read, 'Moses the servant of the LORD died there in Moab, as the LORD had said. He buried him in Moab, in the valley opposite Beth Peor, but to this day no one knows where his grave is.' But it is thought that the writer of *The Assumption of Moses*, with claimed insight into the angelic realm, embroidered the scriptural facts. He imagined, perhaps reasonably, that Satan wanted the site of Moses' grave to be known because he knew that if it was known, it would become a snare to the people. It would draw Israel to hold that place in great reverence and cause it to become a centre of idolatry. The tale therefore explains that the archangel Michael contended with Satan over this. But the point is this: Jude says that the writer of *The Assumption of Moses* explains that, as the archangel contended with the devil, he did not use abusive words even against Satan, but said, 'The Lord rebuke you.' If the writer of this literature on which the false teachers partially base their own experiences directs us to the fact that the archangel acknowledged the authority of the Lord, how can these men claim to be spiritual? If *The Assumption of Moses* directs us away from abusiveness even towards the devil, how can these profane men be looked upon as superior or wise? Even their own sources contradict them.

There is a second way of taking the story which ends at the same point basically, but focuses more on the authority of the law than the authority of the Lord himself. More recent evangelical scholars focus on the fact that what these false teachers are doing, according to verse 4, is changing the grace of God into a licence for immorality. In other words, they are saying God's law doesn't matter once we have been converted. 'We are under grace; we can live as we like. The law of Moses is irrelevant.' The technical term for such teaching is antinomianism — against the law. According to these more recent scholars, the slander against celestial beings is not to be equated with using actual words to revile celestial beings. Rather it has to do with this despising of the law. The law of God was given at Sinai through angels. Paul writes, 'What, then, was the purpose of the law? It was added because of transgressions, until the Seed [Christ] to whom the promise referred had come. The law was put into effect through angels by a mediator' (Gal. 3:19). So angels and the law are very closely intertwined, say these newer scholars. The false teachers were encouraging Christians into immorality and so to reject God's law.

The more recent scholars say the story is actually (and this depends on an understanding of the Greek) that after Moses' death Satan was accusing Moses of his sin, his own law-breaking — for example, in murdering the Egyptian (Exod. 2:12). But, they say, the law of God is so important that not even the archangel Michael could answer Satan and declare Moses forgiven and acceptable. Only the Lord himself can forgive the breaking of his most holy law. Therefore the arch-angel said in effect to Satan, 'The Lord himself rebuke you for the accusations that you make against his servant Moses.' But by rejecting the law as worthless, the false teachers were dis-paraging that which concerned the angels, and obviously tread-ing upon ground into which no man can intrude. By doing that they show that, in fact, they are not wise at all; they are not spiritual as they claim. They are deluded and conceited fools, even in the terms of *The Assumption of Moses*.

Personally, I feel that the view of the older commentators has much to commend it in the context of the rest of Jude and that the interpretation of the more recent scholars seems too contrived. Jude makes no explicit reference to the law of God, and the use of *The Assumption of Moses* seems a very circui-tous route by which to address the problem of straight antinomianism. But either way, the point is the same. These false teachers are not wise in rejecting the authority of the Lord, as they claim. Actually they are spiritually ignorant. It is easy to be taken in by extravagant stories of angelic encoun-ters, or self-inflating talk about freedom in Christ. True spir-ituality is not to do with mere talk, or experiences. It is to do with pleasing God by Christlike character and submissive obedi-ence. We are free in Christ — free not to sin, free to serve. These men are spiritual dunces.

Having begun to show these men for what they are, Jude
now drives home the point: **'These men speak abusively
against whatever they do not understand; and what things
they do understand by instinct, like unreasoning animals
— these are the very things that destroy them'** (v. 10). They
claim to be wise, but in fact they are ignorant. They claim to
be men with enlightened minds, but actually they behave more
like animals. They are dominated by fleshly appetites. In their
sexual immorality they are like horses or dogs on heat, unable
to control their desire. Such behaviour will bring down the
judgement of God and destroy them, just as Jude has explained
in verses 5-7.

It is worthwhile knowing that, not only did popular thinking associate angels with the stars, but also that chapter 86 of
The Book of Enoch speaks of a star falling from heaven and
being transformed into bulls, who then impregnate other animals. This again fits so well here with Jude's description. If
the false teachers did see themselves as some kind of angelic
beings for whom immorality was legitimate, they may well
have based their teaching on such a passage. But Jude, in verse
10, is turning the tables on them and proclaiming that all they
are is 'unreasoning animals'.

Think about it. This has parallels in our own day. So many
so-called radical Christian groups and strutting TV evangelists have fallen into immorality. They say they want people's
souls, but actually they are after people's bodies. So many of
the so-called 'word-faith' teachers claim to have had visions
and talked to angels and met the Lord themselves. But when it
comes to it in their ministry, what are they after? They are
after your money. They press you to fill the collection plate.
What a low, base thing! It may come wrapped up in all sorts of
spiritual claims and supernatural stories, but actually it is just
the old covetousness. It claims to be spiritual, but deep down

it is motivated by the flesh. 'I want your money.' Identify such people and reject them.

Paul Johnson's book entitled *The Intellectuals* made the headlines when it was first published a few years ago. Though its author's own reputation has fallen since then, no one disputes the facts that he has brought to light. In the book he gives something of the histories of many of the great men who have shaped modern thinking. He deals with people like Karl Marx and Rousseau. He documents how nearly every single one of them were immoral men, breaking their marriage vows, or cheating in various ways. They all made various kinds of claims about the truth and what is or is not reasonable and rational. These are the children the Enlightenment, but actually they were just making a way for themselves to pursue their own lusts. These men who made so much of their intellect actually behaved like unreasoning animals. So don't be taken in. Identify and reject such people. They claim to be wise, but in fact they are full of spiritual ignorance. The lustful desires which they pursue, cloaked in a show of enlightened understanding, will actually destroy them, and you if you follow them. Following them inevitably leads to destruction because they are going after sin, which is like high explosive that cannot be defused. It will blow you up. Only Christ and his cross can defuse it. That is the ignorance of the false teachers.

The variety of the false teachers (v. 11)

But then Jude moves on a stage. He wants to point out just how dangerous these specific false teachers are and how virulent is their error. He does so by declaring that they encapsulate all the worst possibilities of false teachers. Again Jude uses a threesome: **'Woe to them! They have taken the way**

of Cain; they have rushed for profit into Balaam's error; they have been destroyed in Korah's rebellion.' We should not be following such men; we should be lamenting the terrible end to which they are travelling. All that is worst about three famous characters from the Old Testament, Cain, Balaam and Korah, finds expression in these particular false teachers.

In explaining this, of course, Jude is implying that there are different types of false teachers of which we need to be aware. Some are like Cain; some are like Balaam; some are like Korah; some are a combination of some or all such heretics. We fall into a great trap if we think all false teachers are of the same kind. Jude identifies for us three different types of false teachers here. Let us look at each one of them briefly.

Cain

First of all, he brings us back to Cain, Adam's son who opposed his brother Abel: **'They have taken the way of Cain.'** In directing our attention to Cain, Jude is telling us that false teachers have been around right from the beginning of time, so we should not be surprised that they are with us today. What does the Bible tell us about Cain, Adam's son? We are told, in Genesis 4, that the two brothers brought offerings to the Lord. Abel gave an offering to the Lord and the Lord accepted it, but Cain's offering was rejected. This angered Cain and he killed Abel. When asked by God where his brother was, Cain replied with unconcern, 'I don't know. Am I my brother's keeper?' How are these facts about Cain interpreted in the New Testament?

In Hebrews chapter 11 we find something of the contrast between Cain and Abel: 'By faith Abel offered God a better sacrifice than Cain did. By faith he was commended as a righteous man, when God spoke well of his offerings. And by faith he still speaks...' (Heb. 11:4). How did it come about that Cain's offering was rejected and Abel's was accepted? Because Abel offered what he offered in faith. The implication is that Cain did not have faith. He did not trust God. So that is the first thing we know about Cain: he had *no faith*.

Secondly, John tells us: 'This is the message you heard from the beginning: We should love one another. Do not be like Cain, who belonged to the evil one and murdered his brother. And why did he murder him? Because his own actions were evil and his brother's were righteous' (1 John 3:11-12). Here is the next thing that we learn about Cain. We should love another and not be like Cain, who had *no love*.

If we put those things together, no faith and no love, what do we have? We have an unconverted man here. Faith and love are the great signs of spiritual life. Paul tells us that the only thing that really matters about a person is faith expressing itself through love (Gal. 5:6). Cain is not a converted man. Cain is a picture of the unconverted church leader or religious teacher. Sadly, it appears there are many such people in our religious education departments at colleges and our theology faculties at universities and in high-ranking clergy positions of establishment churches. They are leaders who have gone into these places as a career and they have come to prominence. Perhaps they are very highly educated, with many degrees after their names, but they are not saved. They have never submitted themselves to the Lord, confessing their sin and crying out for regeneration and for a new heart. Thus they lead people astray. Thus they have no love for God's people. Thus they take his Word and think that simply by pure intellect they can understand it, when actually they need the enlightenment of his Spirit. Very often, in a way similar to Cain's hatred of Abel, it is these people who are the most belligerent in their denunciation of the authority of the Bible and of those who preach faith alone in Christ alone and the gospel of grace. This is the way of Cain. Know what the Scripture says. Identify these men and reject them. That is the first variety of false teacher.

Balaam

Then we come to a second type of false teacher, Balaam. He is quite a different man. **'Woe to them! They … have rushed for profit into Balaam's error.'** You could not accuse him of being unspiritual. Here is a man with some kind of spiritual power, able to prophesy the future, able to bless and curse. We can read all about this in Numbers 22-24. When God rescued Israel out of slavery in Egypt he enabled them to defeat anyone who stood against them in their march to the promised land. Seeing this, King Balak of Moab was terrified, yet at the same time was determined to resist Israel. He decided to avoid military action; instead he looked for someone who could put a curse on God's people. He turned to Balaam and promised him a large reward if he would curse Israel. A man with some strange and wonderful spiritual gift, Balaam seemed to know God and God spoke to him. Yet such was his desire for money that when the Lord said he could not curse Israel, Balaam said, 'Well, couldn't I? Yes, go on, let me do it.' For the love of money, he compromised his status. For the love of the honour Balak had promised him, he disobeyed the Lord. Yes, he did have some kind of relationship with the Lord, but compromised his whole spirituality through the love of money.

We read elsewhere in the Scriptures that Balaam actually told the enemies of Israel how to bring Israel down. This is indicated in Revelation 2:14 as the Lord speaks to the church in Pergamum: 'Nevertheless, I have a few things against you: You have people there who hold to the teaching of Balaam, who taught Balak to entice the Israelites to sin by eating food sacrificed to idols and by committing sexual immorality.' There are many who seem to start out as sincere Christian preachers — often they are men of gifts and ability — but through the love of this world, they go off the rails. Sometimes they are men around whom miraculous things appear to happen. They are frequently men whom church-goers love to listen to and somehow, through the attention and flattery they receive, their heads are turned.

Perhaps I need to underline this point. God warns us in Deuteronomy that there will be such people: 'If a prophet, or one who foretells by dreams, appears among you and announces to you a miraculous sign or wonder, and if the sign or wonder of which he has spoken takes place...' (Wow! This is happening and people are impressed!) '...and [if] he says, "Let us follow other gods" (gods you have not known) "and let us worship them," you must not listen to the words of that prophet or dreamer. The LORD your God is testing you to find out whether you love him with all your heart and with all your soul' (Deut. 13:1-3). Here is a different sort of false teacher from Cain. He has amazing powers, it seems, but is calling people away from the Scriptures, away from godliness. Identify such people and reject them. That is the second type of false teacher.

Korah

Korah was among the Levites appointed by Moses to help with the service of God in the tabernacle. You can read the story in Numbers 16. But despite his position Korah was responsible for provoking rebellion against the leadership of Moses and Aaron. It is interesting that this rebellion is documented after an incident where God told Moses that a man who had broken the Sabbath had to be put to death, and that the Israelites needed to wear tassels on the corners of their garments in order to help them to remember God and his laws.

These moves seem to have brought to the surface grudges against Moses and Aaron which had been festering in Korah and about 250 others. They came to Moses and Aaron and protested, 'You have gone too far!'

Under a cloak of standing for egalitarianism among God's people, Korah questioned the leadership of Moses and Aaron: 'Aren't all the people of God holy? What are you doing telling us what God wants?' He encouraged the Levites to complain, 'Why can't we be priests? Why can't we do what you and Aaron do?' Under this guise of egalitarianism, he provoked discontent and it would seem actually desired that leadership for himself. If Cain was unbelieving and Balaam loved money, Korah loved power and position. His rebellion was prompted by the idea that leadership among God's people is something to which we can appoint ourselves. This is not true. It is God who chooses leaders, gifting them and anointing them. Moses responded to Korah's challenge, not by throwing his own weight around, but by humbly assembling the people and calling God to show whom he had chosen. God intervened in judgement and the ground opened and swallowed up the rebels as they stood together opposing Moses and Aaron.

There have always been such self-opinionated trouble-makers among God's people and in the churches. Often they are younger people, 'men in a hurry' to make it to what they see as 'the top' in Christian circles. They are motivated by jealousy, by a lusting after position and a desire to be seen. They are frequently opportunists who capitalize on difficult times to undermine God's appointed leaders. Here are solid, experienced Christian, evangelical leaders who have led well, but up come these new upstarts and they start casting aspersions: ' Old-fashioned!' 'Yesterday's men.' 'Bad decision!' 'Self-appointed!' 'Let the young people lead!' Sometimes older leaders can be too keen to hold on to their office and refuse to make way for a younger generation. This is wrong. But a God-appointed up-and-coming leader will find a gracious way of coping with that situation. He will not follow Korah's rebellion. Beware of troublemakers like Korah. Identify them and reject them. **'They have been destroyed in Korah's rebellion.'** Jude's words imply that such people are as good as judged already. This is an indication that although false teachers make a big impact, often they do not last for long.

We have people of all these different varieties around today, men like Cain, Balaam and Korah. Jude's words imply that the false teachers whom he was confronting showed elements of every one of these in their character and ministry. Jude's three types of false teacher are probably not meant to be an exhaustive list. There are other types too. We are to test all teachers by their doctrine and their life. True Christian leadership is humble service out of devotion to the Lord Jesus Christ. The Lord told his quarrelling, ambitious disciples, 'Whoever wants to become great among you must be your servant, and whoever wants to be first must be slave of all. For even the Son of Man did not come to be served, but to serve, and to give his life as a ransom for many' (Mark 10:44-45).

The effects of the false teachers

We have seen something of the ignorance of false teachers and the types of false teachers; now Jude gives a list of some of the effects produced by false teachers: **'These men are blemishes at your love feasts, eating with you without the slightest qualm — shepherds who feed only themselves. They are clouds without rain, blown along by the wind; autumn trees, without fruit and uprooted — twice dead. They are wild waves of the sea, foaming up their shame; wandering stars, for whom blackest darkness has been**

reserved for ever' (vv. 12-13). Here Jude uses a wealth of damning illustrations to shock our imaginations. He wants to set us on full alert concerning these false teachers, and the best way to do that is to bring before us six almost nightmare pictures which we shall find hard to forget. He uses two human illustrations — a bride's beauty and a shepherd's work. He follows this with four illustrations from nature — clouds, trees, waves and stars.

A bride's beauty

False teachers disfigure the church. **'These men are blemishes at your love feasts.'** The church is frequently called the bride of Christ in Scripture. Her loveliness consists of her faith and fidelity to the Lord Jesus. Here is a beautiful girl, lovely to look upon. But along comes dreadful a accident. Perhaps it is a car accident, or she is burned badly in a fire, or she suffers some horrific attack, and she is terribly scarred. This is the effect of false teaching on Christ's bride. Through immorality the beautiful Cinderella is turned into the ugly sister.

The love feasts of the church were a combination of a fellowship meal and a communion service, where God's people had fellowship with each other and with the Lord. They are described as **'eating with you without the slightest qualm'**. That word 'qualm' is better translated 'fear' or 'reverence'. They are men who boastfully see themselves as an élite. Even immorality is not seen as a sin to them. Their arrogant claims about themselves leave no room for awe and thankfulness for the Lord who has given his body and blood to redeem us. The very presence of these men in such meetings is both offensive to the Lord and dangerous to the Christians. No doubt these men could be affable and persuasive, and so their ways could easily rub off onto others around them. They are 'blemishes', or scars, on the face of Christ's bride. False teachers are the drunk drivers and the vicious rapists of the church. Thank the Lord that he can heal his bride, and make us beautiful again as we repent.

A shepherd's work

Teachers and leaders are the shepherds and carers of God's people. But these false teachers are **'shepherds who feed only themselves'**. Their so-called ministry is actually just manipulation for their own good. They say what people want to hear in order to get people under their power, and to take from them. Jude is probably alluding to Ezekiel 34:2-4: 'Woe to the shepherds of Israel who only take care of themselves! Should not shepherds take care of the flock? You eat the curds, clothe yourselves with the wool and slaughter the choice animals... You have not strengthened the weak... You have not brought back the strays or searched for the lost.' The false shepherds make their own lives comfortable, while avoiding the hard graft and arduous tasks of the true shepherd. Their view of the grace of God is that it gives us opportunity to serve sin and self rather than God (v. 4). It should not surprise us if this is reflected in their personal ministry.

The clouds

Next Jude turns to two pictures from nature to show the pretentious uselessness of the false teachers. The first is this: **'They are clouds without rain, blown along by the wind.'** They promise so much, but do not deliver. The land of Palestine is hot. The need for rain to make the land thrive and produce crops is obvious. One thinks about the drought of Elijah's day and how everyone longed for rain. Imagine the excitement of waking up one morning in the middle of that drought and seeing clouds on the horizon. 'Perhaps there will be refreshing

rain for the thirsty land after all!' But imagine the disappoint-
ment and frustration when those same clouds blow quickly
over, and no rain falls. False teachers promise so much. Usually their promises are shaped by the prevailing winds of worldly
desires and thinking. They can often appear so relevant. But
the prevailing winds of this world never bring the cloud of
God's glory and grace which alone can refresh weary souls.

The fruit trees

If the false teachers do not bring refreshment, neither do they
produce the fruit God is looking for. They are **'autumn trees,
without fruit and uprooted — twice dead'**.

I was in Kenya a few years ago. I had also been there three
summers before. Nairobi has many, many so-called evangelical conventions. On my last visit, there were great posters
proclaiming meetings under the banner 'Holy Ghost Explo-
sion!' Sadly, there had been similar posters there three years
before, but the country was precisely the same and so was the
city. Great big promises were made, but when you look, nothing
has changed, nothing has happened. The fruit which God longs
to see is the fruit of holy lives, lovingly devoted to the service
of our Saviour. But false teaching always produces false lives.
Again this should not surprise us with reference to the false
teachers Jude is opposing. If their gospel is that God's grace
legitimizes sin, or brings self-fulfilment, making us like 'gods',
is it any wonder if it produces not God-centred, but self-centred
people?

Jesus tells us to measure teachers, true or false, by the fruit
they produce in their own lives and the lives of their hearers.
We are to look at the effects they produce. Autumn should be
the time when a tree's fruit is ripe for the picking. But the false
teachers are fruitless because they are doubly dead. They are

trees which are naturally barren and, anyway, they have been uprooted from the soil of Christ, who alone can make us fruitful.

The sea

It is not just that these teachers are failing to produce godly fruit; they are positively besmirching the church: **'They are wild waves of the sea, foaming up their shame.'** If you go down to the seashore on a winter's day sometimes in the great storms the waves crash against the coast and they throw up the shale right over the land. It cascades onto the shore, right up onto the beaches and beyond. And whatever flotsam and jetsam, whatever rubbish, there is in the sea is dumped up onto the land. These false teachers, with all their great so-called energy and all their great claims, are throwing up rubbish onto the church.

Sorrowfully we have to say that the evangelical church in the West has been drifting from biblical Christianity and biblical standards for many years now. In the USA we have seen the false teaching of 'easy-believism', which turns God's grace into an opportunity for moral laxity, proclaimed by TV evangelists for years, and many of those evangelists have themselves fallen into immorality or grave financial fraud. Mud has been thrown onto the church and the name of Christ. In Britain, at a large, well-known set of Christian conferences in 1995, young people from Christian backgrounds were interviewed and that census found that church young people generally were as much involved in the drug culture as their worldly counterparts. It is absolutely shameful that this should be the case. Here is the result of trendy teaching which makes the grace of God a doorway to laxity and worldliness. The old biblical paths of being straight and plain about morality and giving ourselves to a daily quiet time and living in a way that is different from the world has been scorned as out of date. This is the result of that. Don't blame the youngsters. In a real sense it is not their fault. It is the sway that false teaching has had in the churches.

The stars

What effect will their false teaching have on the teachers themselves? The false teachers' destiny is finally mentioned: **'wandering stars, for whom the blackest darkness has been reserved for ever'**. Jude takes up a dangerous analogy here. He likens the false teachers to stars followed by astrologers. People read the stars and think that in this way they can find wisdom and fortune. Perhaps Jude uses this analogy because in ancient thinking, especially the kind of thinking associated with *The Book of Enoch,* angels and stars were thought to be closely related. Perhaps it was thought that by reading the stars one could read the wisdom of the angels and these false teachers compared themselves to angels. Perhaps the false teachers preached and promoted themselves as 'stars' who could bring spiritual enlightenment to others. But there is only one star which brings true light and that is the Lord Jesus (Num. 24:17), who is the bright Morning Star (Rev. 22:16). To reject him as sovereign and Lord, as the false teachers had done, means not only to be a false guide to others, but to end in the darkness of hell oneself.

All this is a sober message, isn't it? We have seen the ignorance of false teachers, despite their great claims to wisdom, the different types of false teachers and the effects that false teachers have on Christ's pure bride. These things leave us disturbed and shocked. But the main lesson is plain. What is the quickest way to ruin the church? It is simply to believe that false teaching does not matter.

5.
Prophecy about false prophets

Please read Jude 14-19

People are sometimes told that they are paranoid. What is paranoia? Well, the jokey way of explaining it is rather like this: 'I told my psychiatrist that everyone hates me. He said that I was being ridiculous — everyone hasn't met me yet!' That is paranoia. It is a fixed delusion that everyone is out to get us, that everyone is against us.

With all the warnings in Jude of false teachers and the corruption that is threatening the churches as he writes this letter, it would be easy for his Christian readers to become paranoid, or at least fearful and discouraged. 'Look at the false teachers! They seem to be everywhere. They have such influence. They are targeting us. There is no hope for the gospel!' But Jude is a good shepherd. He is concerned not to leave his readers fearful and downhearted as believers. So, in verses 14-19, he wants to bring them something to encourage them and to help them get things in perspective.

What he does, therefore, is to bring two predictions concerning the destiny of the false teachers. The false teachers are called 'these men' throughout verses 8-19. 'These dreamers' (v. 8) say they are having new revelations from the Lord. With their prophetic utterances, they claim the Lord is telling them this and telling them that in their dreams. These supposed revelations are contrary to the apostolic faith given to us in

Scripture. 'Well,' says Jude, 'the ones who have been making prophecies have been prophesied about themselves.' These men who make their false predictions have themselves been predicted. The false teachers have themselves been the subject of God's teaching to us. The Lord knows all about them.

Although it may be very difficult in the heat of the battle with false teachers, when all kinds of rumours abound and trouble is breaking on the church, Jude says to us, 'Look, get it in perspective, it is a very dangerous situation, but it is not out of God's control. He is still on the throne.' Therefore, when we face false teaching, although there is a need to be careful and tough, there is no need to despair; there is no need to become paranoid as Christians.

If you look back, you see that what he is actually doing is almost expounding what he said at the beginning of verse 4: 'For certain men whose condemnation was written about long ago have secretly slipped in among you.' They have used great subtlety and stealth. Their plans were secret to you at that point, but they were known to God. They and their kind were known to God long, long ago, and God has predicted their coming and their condemnation. Therefore get things in perspective. That is the main point of this section.

Now verses 14-19 split into two sections. First, in verses 14-16, Jude reminds them of the opening prophecy from *The Book of Enoch*. Then in verses 17-19, we have the prediction from the apostles of Christ.

Before we examine the text in detail we might ask why he chooses these two sources for his argument at this point. The answer is probably, as I have already indicated, that the false teachers have thrown such aspersions on Christ and the churches have been filled with such doubts that, although the content of what Jude says here is certainly scriptural, he has felt it best to be more subtle in the way it is packaged. He is using these sources to get past his readers' defences.

The prophecy of Enoch

So let's look first of all at the prophecy of Enoch. Jude writes, **'Enoch, the seventh from Adam, prophesied about these men: "See, the Lord is coming with thousands upon thousands of his holy ones to judge everyone, and to convict all the ungodly of all the ungodly acts they have done in the ungodly way, and of all the harsh words ungodly sinners have spoken against him"'** (vv. 14-15).

This is more or less a direct quotation from *The Book of Enoch* chapter 1:9. Now, as I have argued already, there is no reason to necessarily jump to the conclusion that Jude accepts the prophecy of Enoch given here as Scripture. But there are a number of matters to bear in mind.

Firstly, there seems a cogent argument to believe, as has been outlined earlier, that *The Book of Enoch* (with its lists of names of celestial beings, its angelic encounters and conversations) would be the kind of literature preferred by the false teachers against whom Jude is writing. Therefore to answer them in terms of their own sources makes sense. It may well be, in the light of verse 4, that the false teachers did not recognize the authority of Christ (who is the key to understanding the Scriptures) and therefore Jude seeks to first refute them on their own ground.

Secondly, we have to say that the contents of this particular quotation from *The Book of Enoch* can be reconstructed as a pastiche of verses from the canonical Old Testament Scriptures. Without any distortion of the basic intention of the passages, Moses' prayer for Israel in Deuteronomy 33:2-4 together with the words of Isaiah 66:15-16 and Malachi 3:13 virtually cover the whole text. So, in a sense, Jude can justify his quotation as Scripture. Indeed, such Old Testament scriptural references may well have been the original texts from which the writer of *The Book of Enoch* drew his inspiration for this part of his work.

Thirdly, as we shall see later, although we may not have realized it, there is recorded in Scripture a prediction of the judgement of ungodliness by Enoch. Putting all this together gives complete legitimacy to Jude's use of the quotation without having to believe that Jude regarded *The Book of Enoch* as Scripture.

Whatever is the truth about how Jude came to use the words he did, for those of us with faith in the Bible as God's Word Matthew Henry's commentary sums it up succinctly. There we read, 'This prophecy of Enoch, we have no mention made of in any other part or place of the Scriptures, yet now it is Scripture!' In one sense, that indeed is the end of the argument.

Enoch appears in Genesis 5:21-24. The great feature of his life was that he walked so closely with God by faith that he did not see death, but was transported straight to heaven, as is explained in Hebrews 11:5. It is probably this scriptural fact of the transportation of Enoch immediately into the heavenly realms which provoked the imagination of the writer of *The Book of Enoch* to embroider his fictional stories of Enoch's supposed earlier celestial adventures.

Jude describes Enoch as **'the seventh from Adam'**. He is the seventh from Adam in the genealogical lists, such as 1 Chronicles 1:1-3, if we include both Adam and Enoch in our counting. This could simply be to distinguish him from another Enoch, Cain's son, mentioned in Genesis 4:17. But it is more likely that it is meant to remind Jude's readers that the false teachers attached some kind of mystical significance to such numbering. Jude is then implying, 'If these false teachers attach such significance to this man Enoch, then they ought to listen to what their material says that he prophesied about ungodliness.' Terrible judgement awaits all ungodliness. This is Jude's reason for using this quotation.

Sin is obviously tempting. It appeals to the fallen nature in us. Therefore, when tempted, we go through a great struggle.

We want to go God's way if we are really Christians and yet the devil, who is so subtle, holds out these enticements which so appeal to our lower nature, to our flesh. We feel ourselves torn one way and the other. We are sometimes in the middle of a struggle between the spirit and the flesh. We feel there is a war going on inside us and the conflict can be dreadful. If there is false teaching in the church which gives the green light to sin, that sense of struggle is heightened even further. When we are in that situation, we need to have our minds powerfully addressed by the truth, by scriptural truth. That is such a great help. We need to be shown things clearly and in bold colours because, of course, the devil puts out the bait but he doesn't show us the hook. He never tells you the complete truth about where sin leads, does he? He holds out the subtle temptation but he hides the results of sin.

Now here Jude is dealing pastorally with people who are in the thick of the battle. The false teachers were right in the church, dangling immorality in front of them and saying, 'It's all right to do this as a Christian. Go on and do it. It's OK!' Jude is proclaiming: 'I want you to understand that this is serious. I want you to see that actually these false teachers are going to judgement and if you go with them, you go with them to judgement.' Once we are truly saved we can never be lost. But no one can be so sure that he or she is truly saved as to deliberately choose a sinful lifestyle. In fact, to happily choose such a path is likely to be a sign that you were never saved in the first place. And even if you are a real Christian but you fall into sin and you backslide through this, even though later you come back to the Lord, if you backslide because of these temptations, you are going to lose out too. You are going to make yourself dirty and therefore the Lord is not going to be able to use you and bless you as he would have done.

Let us imagine an example of this. If we have been out on business far away and we drive back, arriving home at midnight, we may feel very hungry. So we decide it is time for scrambled eggs, or beans on toast, or something like that when we get in. When we get into the kitchen, what are we looking for? We are looking for a clean pan. We might find a pan in the sink with old porridge in it which has been left from breakfast. Well, we are not going to use that one, are we? We are looking for a clean one. The Lord is looking for a clean vessel to use. If we get ourselves mixed up in sin, yes, we may be forgiven (and we shall be forgiven if we are real Christians because we shall repent) but we are not going to be as useful to the Lord. It is the true Christian's greatest delight to know the nearness of the Lord and be useful to him. We are not going to know that blessing that we could have done.

So here Jude is warning, in particular, that these false teachers are going to judgement. Since the beginning of time, since the days of Enoch, just the seventh from Adam, God endorsed holiness as the way to live. Enoch's holy life was so endorsed by God that he did not see death, but was taken immediately to heaven. Indeed we do have a prediction of judgement on ungodliness by Enoch in Scripture, quite apart from *The Book of Enoch*. Enoch named his son Methuselah. The name Methuselah can be translated to mean something like 'Man of the sending forth'. The Puritan commentator Matthew Poole has it as 'He dies, and the sending forth'. If we take the figures concerning life-spans literally in the early chapters of Genesis we find that the year that Methuselah died was the year God sent forth judgement on ungodliness in the Flood. In the name of his son, Enoch had predicted judgement on sinful ways.

The very fact that Enoch gave his son this name implies that he carried a deep conviction about the approach of God's wrath and makes it extremely likely that he would indeed have preached this to his generation. Though Jude quotes from *The Book of Enoch*, in a sense he does not have to. He can quite legitimately, in the light of Scripture, speak of Enoch prophesying judgement on the ungodly.

The point that Jude wants to make concerns the fact that such a prophecy was made so long ago (cf. v. 4). The fact of judgement has been preached since the early years of Genesis. 'Even since *his* day, the judgement and condemnation of ungodliness have been predicted,' Jude is saying, 'so get it clear in your mind as you are tempted. Be absolutely clear. This is coming. How utterly foolish therefore these false teachers are! It has been predicted for so long, and yet they are going on in their false teachings. How foolish they are! Do not follow them.' Further, he is telling his readers not to become discouraged. God has had his eye on these false teachers for a long time.

Lessons about coming judgement

Using the quotation from *The Book of Enoch,* Jude tells us five scriptural truths about this judgement.

Certain judgement

The opening words of the prophecy tell us, **'See, the Lord is coming.'** Judgement is not an event which may or may not happen. The Lord is pictured, in many Scriptures, as already on his way to judge. When we look at history through the spectacles of Scripture we see that God has poured out his judgements again and again through history. Judgement is something he is continually involved in. These temporal judgements which we see in this world are, in the imagery of Revelation, the trumpets along the way warning us to get ready as God progresses towards the coming final judgement.

Judgement Day is certain. It is on God's calendar. He is on his way and will not change his mind.

Angelic judgement

Secondly and interestingly, Jude tells us that when the Lord comes he brings a judgement by angels: **'The Lord is coming with thousands upon thousands of his holy ones'** (v. 14). The Lord is the Judge but the angels are used by the Lord as his instruments. The angels who assisted God to give his law at Sinai will also accompany God in judging the lawbreakers. How poignant it is that these false teachers who have been slandering celestial beings (v. 8) are going to be judged by celestial beings! The very ones they have arrogantly abused are the ones who are coming with God to judge the world and to judge them.

Of course, this teaching of angelic judgement is not just found in Jude. It is taught throughout the New Testament.

The Lord Jesus told us that it is a judgement by angels. We can see this in Matthew, in the parable of the wheat and the tares: 'The Son of Man will send out his angels, and they will weed out of his kingdom everything that causes sin and all who do evil. They will throw them into the fiery furnace, where there will be weeping and gnashing of teeth' (Matt. 13:41).

The apostle Paul underlines precisely the same thing when he writes to the Thessalonians, 'This will happen when the Lord Jesus is revealed from heaven in blazing fire with his powerful angels. He will punish those who do not know God and do not obey the gospel of our Lord Jesus' (2 Thess. 1:7-8).

Similarly, in the book of Revelation, the apostle John shows us the bowls of God's wrath being poured out on the sinful world by angels (Rev. 16:1-4,8,10,12,17). How this should make us ponder the horror of the nature of sin! Scripture tells us that God's angels love to be about their business of looking after God's redeemed people (Heb. 1:14). Without sin, no doubt, it would be their joy to so serve all mankind. But these glorious spirits who love to benefit men and women now engage in the terrible judgement of people and they do so not unwillingly, but knowing that judgement is right. What a hellish plague sin is, which turns the love of the angels into abhorrence! So it is a judgement by angels — that is the second point Jude makes.

Universal judgement

Thirdly, he tells us that it is a judgement on all. He comes **'to judge everyone, and to convict all the ungodly'**. There is a tendency in some people to think that 'Yes, perhaps God will judge, but not me. Somehow I will be the exception.' Sometimes people who have been rich and privileged in this world are inclined to think that they will enjoy similar privileges in the next. They are fooling themselves. Certainly these false teachers whom Jude is opposing set themselves up as being an élite group. 'Oh well, God might judge others,' they may well have thought, 'but we are above that.' 'No,' says Jude, 'the Lord is coming to judge everyone.' The book of Revelation particularly underlines this: 'I saw the dead, great and small, standing before the throne, and books were opened' (Rev. 20:12). The well-known, famous faces — they will be there. Small folk who have lived humble lives that no one has heard of — they too will be there, says the book of Revelation. 'The dead were judged according to what they had done as recorded in the books. The sea gave up the dead that that were in it, and death and Hades gave up the dead that were in them, and each person was judged according to what he had done' (Rev. 20:12-13).

Perhaps someone has died at sea in some very far away, unknown place. Perhaps the body has been lost and no one knows about where it is. But God knows and that person will stand before the judgement, says the Scriptures. It is a judgement to judge everyone. We are all sinners. And there is only safety by faith in Jesus Christ, in Christ who himself at Calvary took the judgement we deserve. And if you trust Christ, you will be seeking (you won't always succeed, but you will be seeking) to live a holy life. It is not your holiness that saves you; it is Christ who saves you, but you will be seeking to go his way.

Spiritual judgement

It is, fourthly, a judgement for ungodliness. The root of all moral failure ultimately goes back to a breakdown in our spiritual relationship with God. Notice how in verse 15 that word 'ungodly' keeps popping up all the time. You almost want to say to the writer of this verse, 'Haven't you got another adjective you can use?' But he repeats it, four times in our translation, three times in the Greek: **'to convict all the *ungodly* of all the *ungodly* acts they have done in the *ungodly* way, and of all the harsh words *ungodly* sinners have spoken…'** To be ungodly is to live without God.

This word should also sound an alarm-bell to all respectable unconverted people. Faith in God is relegated to a merely private matter in our post-modern age. But Scripture says that Judgement Day will make it an intensely public matter. Here is the sentence: 'You may be very moral, very well thought of by your friends, but God is not in your life — you are ungodly. You have done many relatively good things, but not for the love of God, not for the glory of God — you are ungodly. You have not done these things for the praise of your Creator, but for lesser reasons, perhaps for your own reputation — you are ungodly. You live without ever acknowledging your true King. You are guilty of cosmic high treason — ungodliness.'

Judgement is falling on ungodly people whether they are respectable, whether they are outwardly religious, or whether they are wanton. The only safety is in Christ.

But it is likely that Jude also focuses on this passage from *The Book of Enoch* and on this word 'ungodliness' because, in their inflated views of their spiritual status, rejecting Jesus Christ as the only Sovereign and Lord and substituting their own teaching for his, perhaps the false teachers saw themselves as in some sense being 'gods'. Yet this is, by definition, ungodly.

At a practical level people can see themselves as 'gods' in different ways. It may come through exalted spiritual experiences which fool them into seeing themselves as gods. It may come through the exalting of human intellect which comes to set itself over against God's Word and to despise Scripture. But, for whatever reason, to see yourself as an autonomous, self-fulfilling being, setting aside the faith once for all entrusted to the saints by God's Son Jesus, is to reject the authority of God over you. This is the very essence of ungodliness. The false teachers appeared so spiritual, but their spirituality disguises the deepest ungodliness, which will be judged.

Truthful judgement

Not only is it a certain judgement by angels, and a judgement on all for ungodliness, it is a judgement in truth. Notice, in verse 15, it is **'to judge everyone, and to *convict* all the ungodly'**. He convicts them as well as judging them. When the Lord comes, all the truth will be exposed. Everything will be open; every deception will be unravelled and seen for what it is. And not only every deception, but every self-deception, will be unravelled. One of the greatest problems with us sinners is that we are self-deceived. We suppress the truth (Rom. 1:18). One of our favourite strategies to accomplish that is to compare ourselves with other people. Though our conscience shouts our sin, we muffle its voice by looking at others and arguing that we are not so bad as they. Foolishly, of course, we forget that they too are sinners, so our comparison means nothing. It is the slime calling the mud filthy. It is self-deception.

But God's judgement enlightens us to the truth about ourselves. Every pretence and every hidden motive, including those which we have hidden from ourselves, will come to the surface so that when God condemns, all who are condemned, without exception, will hang their heads and know that God is right to condemn them. They will be convicted. They will acknowledge that God is right. So it is a judgement in truth.

At the moment, people come with all kinds of arguments as to why God is all wrong to judge, but they will not on that day. On that day, his light will burst upon us and it will be obvious as to why he is right to judge us. It is a judgement in truth. Everything will be laid bare and every convicted person will know that what God is doing is just. These false teachers who deceived others and deceived themselves will be exposed.

It is a judgement which is certain, a judgement by angels, a judgement on all, a judgement for ungodliness, a judgement in truth. Are you ready for that day? Let me suggest to you what the Lord may ask you on that day. Perhaps you are reading this as a non-Christian. If so, what will he ask you?

I believe the Judge's first question will go something like this: 'Did you make yourself? And the good things in your life — wasn't it obvious that they were a gift to you? Perhaps you have great intellectual ability, athletic ability, or social skills, and other people do not. Why did you have those? Did you give yourself those things, or were they a gift to you?' You will have to confess they were God's gift to you.

Then, perhaps, the second question he will ask you is this: 'Did you not in your own heart often condemn others when they lacked gratitude towards you?' You will hang your head and say, 'Yes, there were many occasions when I did something for somebody and they weren't thankful to me and I went away thinking: "You ungrateful little horror" and I condemned them in my heart because I know that ingratitude is all wrong.'

Then the third question the Lord will ask will be along these lines: 'How has your life shown gratitude to me, your Creator? How has your life given glory to my Son whom I sent to save sinners? How have you responded to my gifts?'

And as those questions are asked in the great courtroom of Judgement Day, we know that without Christ we are condemned, don't we? We know he is right. The truth is exposed. There is only one thing we should do and that is flee to Jesus Christ before that great day comes and cast ourselves upon his mercy. He has died for all our sins, thank the Lord. We can be, and truly are, forgiven. There is only one place of refuge — Jesus Christ. Are you ready for that day?

But instead, of course, the false teachers don't want to know anything about that. They are just using religion for their own ends. Perhaps it is with such thoughts of the questions which God will ask on Judgement Day in mind that Jude goes on to give a brief description of those false teachers.

The false teachers described

In verse 16, he says, **'These men are grumblers and fault-finders; they follow their own evil desires; they boast about themselves and flatter others for their own advantage.'** There is a list of five identification marks on these false teachers.

Grumblers and fault-finders

The false teachers are those who are constantly backbiting against those who preach the truth, like Israel against Moses.

How do they first get a hearing for their false teaching? They
do so by being fault-finders. They search out, and focus on,
the things that are lacking in a church. No assembly of God's
people is perfect this side of glory. Our worship could be improved; our fellowship could be deeper; the leaders would be
the first to acknowledge that they wish they were better at
their work. When we see the blemishes of a church we should
first of all thank God for the positive aspects of the fellowship.
Then we should pray that God would make things better and
lovingly seek to encourage the church in a servant-like spirit.
But these men, when they have found fault, like to whisper
about it to others and grumble. They speak, not to God in
prayer, but to fellow Christians in murmuring. They stir up
discontent.

Following their own desires

In doing this they have an agenda in view. They grumble to
others with the implication that 'We would do things better.
We have the answer.' And so they gain a hearing for their
heresy, and what they have in mind is to gain power for themselves in the church. They do not want to be servants; they
want to be masters. They do not see the church as first and
foremost Christ's church. They see it as something they can
use for their own gratification. Perhaps they justify their attitude to their consciences by telling themselves that 'God wants
me to be happy in my work.' They want to use the church as a
vehicle for their own egos. How will such things look on Judgement Day?

Boasters and flatterers

Their sermons are full of stories about themselves. They boast
of the many conversions; they boast of the number of baptisms;

they tell us all about the number of healings through their ministry. The posters which advertise their crusades say much more about themselves and their name than they do about the name of Jesus Christ. Boasting is always a sign of a false teacher. When Paul confronted such men in his second letter to the Corinthians, the only things he would mention of himself were not his successes, but his weaknesses and sufferings. We follow a crucified Lord who was never a big success in this world's terms.

Not only do they boast, they flatter. Now we must not mix up flattery with encouragement. They are not motivated by a desire to build others up; they are just finding pleasantries to manipulate people. They say things simply to twist people around their little finger and get them going in their direction. They promise young men that they will get them into the ministry. They promise churches that they can see God's blessing coming on them in unimaginable fulness if only they will join their group. They are doing this **'for their own advantage'**. They are building their own empires. How will such things look on the day on which the kingdom of God is revealed? Such men are bound for judgement.

Jude has two messages here that he is underlining. 'Don't follow them,' he is saying. 'They are going to judgement. But also at the same time, do not be unnerved by them. Do not get the trouble they are causing out of proportion. Their doom has been written for many years.'

Now, having predicted the destiny of these men and answered them in their own terms from *The Book of Enoch*, Jude brings the same basic message again, but this time from a different source. He turns to what Christ's apostles have predicted about such false teachers.

The prophecy of the apostles

That Jude does not regard his quotations from the inter-
testamental books as on the same level as Scripture is shown
by the change which occurs in the tone of the language at this
point: **'But, dear friends, remember what the apostles of
our Lord Jesus Christ foretold. They said to you, "In the
last times there will be scoffers who will follow their own
ungodly desires." These are the men who divide you, who
follow mere natural instincts and do not have the Spirit'**
(vv. 17-19).

The appeal, **'my dear friends'**, indicates a major tran-
sition. He is moving away from the half-light of Jewish religious literature into the clear morning of New Testament teaching. It is as if Jude breathes a sigh of relief in the text. Yet at
the same time he presents this apostolic material in a very
shrewd way.

The false teachers, with their dreams and visions, were very
experience-centred in their approach to faith and would have
been encouraging the churches to adopt a similar way of thinking. With this in mind, Jude takes his readers back to their
initial experience of the gospel. He reminds them of the
apostles, who first preached Christ to them and through whom,
if they were true Christians, they were converted, experiencing new birth by the Word of God. The word 'apostle' is used
flexibly in the New Testament. Mostly it refers to the
foundational group of the twelve disciples plus Paul, the special
apostle to the Gentiles. But it can also be used simply to mean
what we would today call a missionary. It may be that the
churches Jude is writing to were planted by the original disciples of Jesus, or it may be that they were planted by lesser-
known men. The main thing is that these people were **'apostles
of our Lord Jesus Christ'**, commissioned by the Lord and
preaching his Word.

Jude reminds his readers of the apocalyptic predictions which were part of the foundational teaching given when the churches came into being. It is startling for us to realize that the apostolic 'follow-up' course for new converts included a grounding in understanding **'the last times'**, and warnings concerning false teachers. However, that this was the case is definitely in line with the tenor of other passages in the New Testament. The apostle Paul, writing his second letter to the Thessalonians, was able to remind them of what he had taught them about the Antichrist and the coming of the 'man of sin'. This thoroughness of teaching is a challenge to the methods of the modern church.

In Scripture, the term 'last times' is almost a technical phrase. The Bible divides the whole of world history basically into two eras. Before the earthly life of the Lord Jesus is designated as 'the former days'. The whole time-period from Christ's ministry, culminating in the Day of Pentecost, right through until his second coming, is called 'the last days' or 'the last times' (Acts 2:16-17; Heb. 1:1-2). Jude and his readers lived in the last times and so do we. This is one of the reasons why what Jude wrote so long ago is still urgently relevant to us today.

The New Testament sees a certain pattern characterizing the whole period from Christ's first to his second coming. During that era the gospel will be preached among the nations (Mark 13:10), but at the same time the church will face many trials, including being deeply troubled by false teachers (Mark 13:5-13). This is what the Lord Jesus predicted, and that same prediction was taught by his apostles. Jude chooses to use the phraseology used by the apostle Peter in 2 Peter 3:3. We have noted earlier the parallel between 2 Peter and Jude and the fact that some scholars are drawn to the idea that Jude acted as Peter's secretary in writing that letter. If this is true, it would be very natural of Jude to turn to this wording. **'They said to**

you, "In the last times there will be scoffers who will follow their own ungodly desires." '

The 'scoffer' is frequently found in the Wisdom literature
of the Old Testament under the term 'mocker' (e.g., Ps. 1:1;
Prov. 1:22). It stands for a person who despises religion and
laughs at morality. Mockers, or scoffers, live loose lifestyles
and make the faith a subject of irreverent humour. In 2 Peter 3
the term seems to refer to more secular people who deride
religion in the name of rationalism. In particular, there they
are seen as having a view of world history which excludes the
supernatural and as those who mockingly reject the idea of
Christ's return. Here in Jude the term is being used of false
teachers who scoff at the faith for different reasons. Certainly
they believe in the supernatural, with their revelatory dreams
and their slandering of angelic beings (v. 8). But they scoff at
the necessity to live a holy life and at the idea that Jesus Christ
is the only Master and Lord (v. 4). Either way, whether from
secularists or from super-spiritual charismatics, Jude is urging
his readers to realize that attacks upon the apostolic gospel
are nothing unusual. They are to be expected. Such things
were predicted by those from whom they had their first experience of the grace of God in the gospel.

The time to worry?

Rather than its making us fearful or paranoid, there is a sense,
paradoxically, in which we can turn the presence of false teachers around to our encouragement. If what Jude is saying is
true, that these things are part of the scriptural pattern of the
last days, then when you see these things, realize that God's
plan is on track. God does foreknow the future and it is coming to pass exactly as he said.

If you were to wake up one morning and everyone pro-
fessed to be a Christian and every church was preaching good,

sound gospel from the New Testament — in a way, that would be the time to worry because that is not what Jesus predicted. If, on the other hand, whenever you turn on your TV, there is an Oxford professor sneering at those who believe in creation, or the BBC social affairs correspondent telling you that divorce has been the greatest liberator in the last 100 years, as it has really freed women (even though everyone knows the damage done to abandoned partners and the children of divorce) you can think to yourself: 'Ah, yes, that is as the New Testament predicted!' When you see politicians who are prepared to use God and to parade their church-going when it is convenient for their career and just to brush it under the carpet or sneer at Christ at other times, you can say to yourself: 'Well, that is what I was to expect. That is what the apostles foretold.' If you see evangelicalism being referred to in the media, and being totally misrepresented, caricatured and demonized, you can come to the conclusion that we are in the last days and it is going the way that the New Testament said it would.

Here is the situation. These are signs of the times. Don't be discouraged. Just realize it is working out. It is a dangerous situation and, in many ways, it is a heartbreaking situation, but it is what is there in the Bible. In fact, in that way, perhaps we could see that the devil (and I say this carefully) is God's fool. When we see what he is doing and we look at the New Testament, we see that the devil actually exposes himself and shows us the reality of the New Testament. In that sense he has actually, as it were, done God's work for him.

There is a great story in the Old Testament, in the book of Esther, of that man Haman who set up a great trap against the Jews and against Mordecai, and who had a great gallows built to hang Mordecai. But he was exposed as a treacherous liar by the gentle wisdom of Esther and he himself was hung on that very gallows! The devil is like that. The devil has all his schemes but actually only hangs himself in the end because God is the sovereign God and God is over all. Therefore, dear

Christian, don't be paranoid; don't be discouraged; be careful and keep looking to the Lord. Keep your eyes on him, keep trusting him.

The false teachers described again

In parallel with what Jude did after quoting the prophecy from *The Book of Enoch*, he now gives us a second description of those false teachers: **'These are the men who divide you, who follow mere natural instincts and do not have the Spirit'** (v. 19).

It may be implied in this verse that the false teachers claimed to have some special gift or anointing of the Holy Spirit. They claimed to have had dreamlike visions and encounters with celestial beings in the spiritual realm. They may well have attributed this to some extraordinary endowment of the Spirit of God. But Jude sees such claims as dangerous nonsense. There are two factors concerning these teachers that make it certain that, for all their claims, they are deceived about their relationship to the Spirit.

Their immoral behaviour

First of all, their immoral behaviour is sufficient evidence that they do not possess the Holy Spirit. They **'follow mere natural instincts'**. The desires of the unregenerate flesh in human beings revolve around sin and self and this world. Sensual pleasure, luxury and immorality are part and parcel with the flesh. The regenerate soul is not immediately perfect, but it does have new desires. These are desires for God, his Word and his worship, for purity of life and loving fellowship. In a word, the work of the Holy Spirit in a truly born-again person is shown by that person's longing to be like Jesus — full of love, joy, peace, patience, kindness, goodness, faithfulness, gentleness and self-control (Gal. 5:22-23). By their desires for money (v. 11), position (v. 16) and legitimizing of immorality (v. 4), they show they do not have the Spirit.

It is worth noting that so many of the debates concerning the church's stance on moral issues in modern times have revolved around what comes 'naturally' to people. 'If I am born with this tendency or "natural instinct", how can it be just for the church to reject my preferred lifestyle, or for me to have to suppress my desires?' Jude's answer is that the life of the church is not about what comes naturally to us; it is about what the Spirit of God can work in us.

They divide the church

The second mark that these false teachers do not have the Spirit is the fact that they disrupt the unity of the church: **'These are men who divide you.'** The word translated 'divide' can mean to separate, or to make a distinction. As this commentary has suggested, the false teachers whom Jude was opposing saw themselves as an élitist group: 'We are a cut above other Christians. We have had some extra blessing that puts us on a different level.' It is unlikely that they were at this point actually leading people out of the church. They were still going to the church's love feasts. However, we can imagine them forming an 'in group' and perhaps even sitting separately from the rest of the brothers and sisters. The implication was, 'We and those who follow us are very, very much better than others.'

They were bringing division where in fact there should not be division, where the people should be moving together as one in the Lord. For all their claims to have great spiritual experiences, Jude says that they 'follow mere natural instincts'. It is interesting that the word he uses there for 'natural' is the word from which we get our word 'psychological'. Their experience is merely psychological; they do not really have the Spirit. How do we know that they do not really have the Spirit? Well, what happened when the Spirit came at Pentecost? Many were converted and they were all joined together as one. They were not divided. Rather, they all came together as one in the apostles' doctrine, the breaking of bread and the prayers and fellowship. They were one, in the truth, in fellowship with one another. That is the work of the Spirit. He brings loving unity in the truth of Christ. But these men love to divide, and make distinctions and to draw off people after them. They do not have the Spirit because they do not 'make every effort to keep the unity of the Spirit through the bond of peace' (Eph. 4:3).

As we look out on our world and the struggles of the churches, especially in the West, we see things which are so similar to those Jude has described that we find it difficult not to think that somehow he had taken a trip in time to the twentieth century. But Jude would say, 'No, it is just that all these things have been predicted long ago.' Therefore Christian, do not become downhearted, or paranoid. Instead we are to take heart!

6.
Taking responsibility for yourself

Please read Jude 20-21

The best way to begin this section is by reminding ourselves that God made us to be active. We have hands and feet. We have eyes to see what should be done, and ears and tongues with which to communicate. God, then, has designed men and women to be doers. And Christianity is not meant to be a spectator sport. We live in an age in which we are encouraged to be spectators. We sit in front of the TV to be entertained. We sit in the north stand of the football stadium and watch the game. And it is tempting to treat going to church on Sunday in the same way — to sit there and watch the performance and then go home. But that is not what we are there for. In many ways it is the very opposite of what Christian meetings should be about. Being in church should actually prepare us for action in the following week. Christianity is not for spectators; it is a faith which encourages us to be up and doing.

In verses 20-23, Jude gives orders concerning what he wants his readers to be doing. He tells us what we ought to be doing for ourselves in verses 20-21 and then he tells us what we ought to be doing for others in verses 22-23. We are going to look at just the first of those sections in this chapter.

Jude is writing the letter, you remember, to stir up Christians to contend for the faith that has been once and for all entrusted to the saints, to the church (v. 3). He is doing that because there are false teachers, bringing lying revelations, who have crept into the church and who have turned the grace of God into an excuse for sin (v. 4). Sadly, at the turn of the second millennium, if we just open our eyes, we can see this happening in many sections of the professing church right now. Certain sections of the professing church are encouraging or allowing all sorts of attitudes and behaviour which has got nothing to do with the New Testament and is way out of line with the will of God. So this letter is very pertinent for us as well. Having described the problem, Jude now tells his readers, 'Don't just sit back — be up and doing something about it.'

The obvious question which they will ask is: 'What should we be doing?' These next verses answer that question. These are the responsibilities he exhorts them to take up: **'You, dear friends, build yourselves up in your most holy faith and pray in the Holy Spirit. Keep yourselves in God's love as you wait for the mercy of our Lord Jesus Christ to bring you to eternal life. Be merciful to those who doubt; snatch others from the fire and save them; to others show mercy mixed with fear — hating even the clothing stained by corrupted flesh'** (vv. 20-23). Those are our responsibilities as Christians. As we have noted, these include first of all responsibilities for ourselves and then responsibilities for others. In this chapter we will focus only on taking responsibility for ourselves.

You have a responsibility for yourself before God. Are you taking responsibility for your own Christian life? False teachers, you know, often like to keep their followers dependent on them. Their followers receive what they think is a blessing, but no more blessing can come unless they turn up at this particular man's meeting next time. 'Oh, I must see the preacher. I saw him last week but I must see him again this week.' And they like to encourage that kind of dependence, of course, because it keeps their followers under their power so they can continue to manipulate them for their own ends. Those ends may be to get more money out of them, or simply to give themselves an ego-trip from the continued adulation. But that is not the way it should be. Good church leaders should be like good parents who are bringing their children to maturity so that they can stand on their own two feet and take responsibility for themselves. If you are really being blessed by God there will be a growing to maturity as a Christian. The Lord Jesus not only called his disciples to follow him; fairly soon he was sending them out on their own missions, so that they would learn to stand and carry on the work after his departure. Every true Christian leader will encourage his flock along the path of maturity and taking responsibility for themselves before God.

Now, here in verses 20-21, there are four key verbs which show us how to take responsibility for ourselves and to grow in maturity. The words are these: 'build', 'pray', 'keep' and 'wait': '*Build* yourselves up in your most holy faith and *pray* in the Holy Spirit. *Keep* yourselves in God's love, as you *wait* for the mercy of our Lord Jesus Christ to bring you to eternal life.' We will explore these verses under the headings of these four key 'doing' words. We are to build, to pray, to keep and to wait.

Build

What is our first responsibility for ourselves? You and I are to be builders: **'Build yourselves up in your most holy faith'** (v. 20). Obviously, the 'most holy faith' is the gospel, that body of truth for which Jude has called us to contend against the heresy of the false teachers.

It is termed 'holy faith' for two reasons. The first is because of *its origins*. This truth has not been thought up by people; it has come from God. It is the good news that the holy God has revealed, which we would never have found out for ourselves, nor could the cleverest people in the world have done so. It has come from heaven. It is a holy faith.

Secondly, this body of truth is known as 'your ... faith' because it is meant to be responded to by us with trust. It is the truth that evokes faith and trust in Jesus Christ and, as we put our faith and trust in him, it changes our lives and cleanses us. So it is 'holy faith' because it has come from God and because of *its results*. It makes us holy. The best way to guard ourselves against the false teaching is to be well acquainted with true teaching. The best way to be inoculated against the immorality of the heretics is to be built up in the truth that leads to godliness. That is our first responsibility.

Now, we are to build ourselves up in that most holy faith. How do we do that? We do it, first, by studying the faith, that is, the Bible; secondly, by believing the Bible; and, thirdly, by obeying the Word of God in the Bible.

Here are some well-known Bible verses that definitely lead us in this direction.

2 Timothy 3:16-17: 'All Scripture is God-breathed and is useful for teaching, rebuking, correcting and training in righteousness.' Why is Paul the writer impressing this on us? He tells us: 'So that the man of God may be thoroughly equipped for every good work.' Why should the Bible be so precious to us? Because through it we can be 'thoroughly equipped', completely equipped, 'for every good work'.

So whether you are a youngster in the faith or someone who has been a Christian for a few years, if you are going along to meetings that are neglecting the Bible or playing the Bible down, or disparaging the Bible as 'God's word for yesterday', you are being led astray. It is through the Scriptures that you will become thoroughly equipped for every good work. You need to be prayerful; you need to be obedient; you need to be believing — all those things as well, but never play down the Scriptures.

Romans 12:1-2: 'I urge you, brothers, in view of God's mercy, to offer your bodies as living sacrifices, holy and pleasing to God — this is your spiritual act of worship. Do not conform any longer to the pattern of this world, but be transformed...' How? '... by the renewing of your mind'. Scripture transforms the mind. Scripture is God's Word, God's thoughts. As we get into Scripture, we begin to think in the way God does and that changes our lives. The mind is the control-room of the human being. If the mind is truly renewed, our affections will be touched, our choices will be different and our whole life will be renewed.

It is not just from religious heretics that wrong ideas are fed to us. All kinds of other ideas come at us, from adverts on TV, things that we read in the bank, brochures from companies that come through the post, magazines we might pick up in the dentist's waiting-room. They fire at us all kinds of ideas about how life is to be lived and what real life is all about. Coca-Cola adverts tell you life is about having fun under blue skies with pretty young women. But that is not life according to the Bible. The building society will tell you that life is about money. The department stores encourage you to think that life is about being smartly dressed. We can easily be dragged along and just get into that way of thinking. When we do, we live no differently from the world. No. Build yourselves up in your most holy faith. Understand the Scriptures. Think God's way and your life will be opened to God's power; it will be transformed and you will be different.

Psalm 1:1-3:

> Blessed is the man
>> who does not walk in the counsel of the wicked...
> But his delight is in the law of the LORD,
>> and on his law he meditates day and night.
> He is like a tree planted by streams of water,
>> which yields its fruit in season
> and whose leaf does not wither.
>> Whatever he does prospers.

This psalm contains a rich promise of blessing through the Word of God. We must *make room* for God's Word by ejecting sin from our lives. Imagine a cup three-quarters full of sand. You will not be able to carry much water in that. You need to empty out the sand first. In just the same way, we must seek to push wrong things out of our lives, reject the way of sin and make room for God's law. We must *make* God's Word *welcome*. We make God's Word welcome when we receive it into our hearts by faith. Without faith we keep God's Word waiting on the doorstep of our lives. We treat it as we would the milkman or the postman rather than as we would a friend. The man in the psalm welcomes God's Word by meditating on it and believingly turning it over and over in his mind. Then we must *make time* for the Word of God. We should listen to it preached in church but, like the man in the psalm who thought on it 'day and night', we should also give time to personal reading and thought. This is the way to be blessed in life.

The prosperous Western church has easy access to the Bible. Living in times when we can always purchase the Bible from almost any bookshop, often we do not treasure the Word of God as we should. With this in mind it is always instructive to understand how Christians under persecution regard the

Scriptures. Here is a snippet from a book by Carl Lawrence writing about past days in China: 'In 1966 the Red Guards made a concentrated effort to burn all Bibles, hymnals and other Christian literature. Today it is not uncommon to see a group of several hundred people with only one Bible. One lady had a complete Old and New Testament. She would bring it to the meeting wrapped in linen. When the pastor read the Scriptures, he would gently take the Bible, carefully unwrap it and read the text. After he was finished, he would return the Bible to the lady and she would wrap it up in linen cloth as others had done to the Lord's physical body. In some houses, certain people are told in advance what Scripture will be needed for the meeting. Each of them will copy one verse and bring it. When the leader wants to lead or speak from Scripture, he collects the handwritten copies, puts them all together and he will have the text. In this way, if the police interrupt the meeting, the Bible will not be lost.'

The Bible is the Word of God written. It is an immense treasure. It encapsulates 'the faith that was once for all entrusted to the saints'. If Jude had lived in our day with the Bible so readily available he would be telling us to study it, to believe it, to obey it. Build yourself up, then, in your most holy faith. That is your responsibility. 'I can't do it for you,' Jude is saying. 'All I can do is exhort you.' Only you can do something about it.

Pray

The second responsibility is to **'pray in the Holy Spirit'** (v. 20).

First of all, before we come to look in detail at what this is really about, I have to ask, are you a prayerful person? Do you pray? Is there a time in the day when you seek God in prayer?

Or are you not a prayerful person at all? You may be in church on Sunday, but is there actually any personal prayer in your life? Then, let me challenge you at another level. Are you at the church prayer meeting? Because the church must be a prayerful people. People who do not pray are practical atheists, no matter what they call themselves. Churches that do not pray are secular organizations, no matter what is stated in their doctrinal basis. Jude challenges us to pray in the context of the dangers of false teaching. Behind false teaching is the great liar, Satan himself. We are no match for the powers of darkness in our own strength, no matter how clever we think we are theologically. Therefore, we must pray. Prayer is not always easy, but nevertheless we must give ourselves to it.

We are called to pray 'in the Holy Spirit'. Some people want to insist that prayer in the Holy Spirit must be prayer in tongues, elsewhere in Scripture called speaking in tongues. I can understand why they say that. I have some sympathy with that. But, with the best will in the world, that cannot be what Jude is talking about here. How do we know that? We know it because 1 Corinthians 12:29-30 makes it clear that not all Christians speak in tongues: 'Are all apostles? ... Do all speak in tongues?' The answer which is definitely expected by the Greek construction is: 'No, not everyone is an apostle. Not everyone does this. Not everyone speaks in tongues.' Not all Christians speak in tongues, or are even meant to speak in tongues. But this command of Jude is a command to all Christians. So he cannot have in mind speaking in tongues, because only some do that according to the New Testament.

What, then, is praying in the Holy Spirit? Let us read about the blessed Holy Spirit in Romans 8:14: 'Those who are led by the Spirit of God are sons of God. For you did not receive a spirit that makes you a slave again to fear, but you received the Spirit of sonship. And by him we cry, "*Abba,* Father." The Spirit himself testifies with our spirit that we are God's children.' The first thing the Holy Spirit gives to a new Christian is a cry. It is a prayer, which is the cry: '*Abba,* Father!' We say to God, 'Father I need you, Father, you are my father!' The Spirit himself lets us know that we have been accepted by God, that we belong to God's family and therefore we can pour out our hearts to him. What is prayer in the Holy Spirit? It is prayer in that spirit of adoption, that spirit of sonship, that coming to the Father through faith in Jesus Christ who has died for us; coming to him pouring out our hearts to him, the depths of our needs and our feelings, as a child would to its father. What is prayer in the Holy Spirit? It is not formal prayer. It is not prayer read mechanically out of a book. It is the prayer of a sincere, regenerated heart, being poured out as a child to the Father in heaven. We are to pray, not with formality and mere outward religion — 'Oh, I pray three times a day,' or whatever the Pharisees did, as they recited their prayers. That is not what Jude is calling us to. Rather, Jude is exhorting us to prayer from a sincere heart, trusting in the Father, inspired by the Spirit of God.

How does the devil stop you praying? Does he tell you that you have got no time? That is one way. One little girl in an interesting Sunday School lesson was once asked, 'If you were the devil how would you stop people praying?' This little girl had an acute mind and a good grasp of spiritual realities. She answered like this: 'If I was in that position, I would use something religious to stop people praying. I would tell people, "You've been to church today. You don't need to pray." I would tell people: "You've read your Bible today. You don't need to pray."' What is the devil using with you to stop you praying? We are to be builders. We are also to be people who pray — prayers. Our struggle is not against flesh and blood, says the New Testament, it is against principalities and powers and wickedness in high places. We need to be engaged in that spiritual battle and in prayer in the Spirit that we might see God to be at work. Don't be a spectator. Don't be someone who just sits there on the terraces on Sunday and then goes away and does nothing about it. Be a player. Be a prayer. Build and pray.

Keep

The third key word is 'keep': **'Keep yourselves in God's love'** (v. 21). The word 'keep', or 'kept', is something of a favourite word of Jude's. There are a number of verses in which he uses it. For example, he writes to those 'who are loved by God the Father and kept by Jesus Christ' (v. 1). The demons that are fallen 'are kept in darkness' (v. 6). Christ the Lord 'is able to keep you from falling' (v. 24). The theme of keeping, or being kept, runs throughout Jude.

Now Jude tells us, **'Keep yourselves in the love of God.'** 'But, hold on,' you might say, 'verse 1 tells us we are being kept as Christians, doesn't it? Well, if we are being kept, why do I need to keep myself?' Human logic would suggest that if God is doing something, then I do not need to do anything about it. But biblical logic is often different. The biblical logic here is that if God is doing something then I should want to do it too. Philippians 2:12,13 is a great classic statement of that kind of thinking: 'Continue to work out your salvation with fear and trembling.' Do something in working out things for yourself as a Christian. Why? 'For it is God who works in you to will and to act according to his good purpose.' Human logic would say, 'If God is doing it, why do I need to do it?' But that is human logic. Biblical logic does not play off the sovereignty of God against the responsibility of man. Instead it emphasizes both equally. Therefore I am to be working out my salvation because God is at work in me. If God is keeping me then it is absolutely right for Jude to say that we must keep ourselves in the love of God. We are to co-operate with what God is doing in our lives. Are you co-operating with the Lord, or fighting against him all the time? How do we keep ourselves in the love of God? To get an insight into this we turn to John chapter 15. There we find the parable that the Lord Jesus uses that he is the vine and we are the branches. We are in him as branches in the vine and so we draw our life from him as we remain in him, as we abide in him. In that passage he says this: 'As the Father has loved me, so have I loved you. Now remain in my love. If you obey my commands, you will remain in my love, just as I have obeyed my Father's commands and remain in his love' (John 15: 9).This verse answers our question. How do we keep ourselves in the love of God? By seeking to obey God and what he has told us through his Son the Lord Jesus Christ. That is how we keep ourselves in the love of God.

In John's Gospel, where the picture of the vine and the branches comes from, the first and main way in which we are to obey God is to have faith in Christ. People asked the Lord, 'What must we do to do the works God requires?' The answer Jesus gave was: 'The work of God is this: to believe in the one he has sent' (John 6:28,29). The false teachers were not only teaching error, but through their error they were encouraging people to redirect their faith away from Christ. But to walk out on Christ is to walk out of the saving love of God. 'Don't do it!' Jude is saying. Keep walking with Christ. As we walk in the path of obedience, we know the smile of God rather than his frown. The immorality into which the false teachers are tempting people in the churches can only bring God's chastisement and, if they reject Christ, his eternal judgement. So Jude calls us, 'Keep yourselves in the paths of the Lord's love. There you will find the Lord's blessings.'

Wait

Fourthly, we are called to wait. We are to build and pray and keep as we **'wait for the mercy of our Lord Jesus Christ to bring you to eternal life'** (v. 21).We are to keep looking forward to the Second Coming, keeping our eyes fixed on Christ, waiting for him.

Many trials, many troubles, come into our lives and those trials and troubles can easily disturb us. The false teachers also try to move us away from Christ. But we must be patient. We must not be moved. We must wait. Sometimes terrible things happen in people's lives and they are tempted to say, 'Well, that's it, I have tried to be a Christian and now the Lord has allowed this to happen in my life and I am walking out on him. I am not waiting for him any more. I'm leaving.' Perhaps you have been tempted like that. Don't do it. Wait. Often false teachers try to capitalize on our trials and troubles. 'You are suffering because you have not discovered the secret we have come to share with you. This old-fashioned Christianity which calls for taking up the cross and enduring hardship is for fools. We can offer you health and wealth now.'

'No,' says Jude, 'do not be taken in. Wait for the Lord.' In particular, we are to wait for his coming. Think about that man in the Old Testament, Joseph. Think about what happened to him. His brothers turn on him. He is sold as a slave into Egypt. When he is there as a slave, a wicked woman accuses him of something he has not done — attempted rape. He is thrown into prison. He languishes in prison for years. He interprets a friend's dream, but when that friend gets out of prison he forgets all about Joseph. How easily Joseph could have said, 'Well, I've tried to trust God, but look what's happened to me. What's the point of going on trusting and believing in him?' But, of course, God had his hand in all this and even through the painful experiences was working a marvellous plan to bring Joseph to that place of great blessing, not just for himself but for his whole family. He is going to rise to become the prime minister of Egypt. Because Joseph waited and did not walk out on God he was blessed. He waited, clung on, even during things that he could not understand.

In just the same way, we are told to wait. We may be in the midst of all kinds of troubles in our personal lives, our family lives, our churches, but we must wait for the mercy of our Lord Jesus Christ to bring us to eternal life. There is something worth waiting for. The world wants everything now; we are to wait. 'You have got trouble and tribulation now in the world. That is just what I had,' says the Lord Jesus to us. 'But you wait. I am risen from the dead and I am coming again. I have heaven for you. Wait for me.' The false teachers were offering the pleasures of sin which last for a short time, but end in destruction. Jude tells us to wait for the Lord Jesus. Such waiting will be rewarded with eternal life and joy.

A thorough Christian

It is worth just bringing together the different aspects of Jude's exhortations in these verses. As we do that we get another lovely answer to the question, 'What is a Christian?' which we asked before in chapter 1. A Christian is one who builds, prays, keeps and waits. A Christian builds his life on the gospel, the Word of God. A Christian prays with the aid of the Holy Spirit. Christians treasure the love God has for us, and keep the flame of love for God burning in their hearts and their lives. Christians are those who look beyond this present life and wait with great expectancy and joy for the coming of the Lord.

This is what we need to be up and doing as Christians, no matter what our circumstances. Let me just illustrate this. Many

Christian brothers and sisters have suffered, and continue to suffer, under Communism in China. I came across the story of a Chinese pastor who had spent eighteen years in prison for his faith. In 1991 he gave this remarkable testimony: 'The authorities put me to work emptying the human waste cesspool. But they did not know in those years how much I enjoyed working there. It was 2 metres square and filled with human waste... I had to walk into the disease-ridden mass and scoop out successive layers... So why did I enjoy working in the cesspool? In the labour camp all the prisoners were normally kept under strict surveillance, but all the guards and prisoners kept a long way off because of the smell. When I worked in the cesspool I could be alone and could pray to the Lord as loudly as I needed. I could recite the Scriptures including all the psalms I still remembered and no one was close enough to protest. I could sing loudly all the hymns I still remembered... Again and again as I sang in the cesspool, I experienced the Lord's presence ... the cesspool became my private garden where I met the Lord.' Through his praying in the Spirit and building himself up in the Scriptures and rejoicing in the love of God the cesspool of the prison became a Garden of Eden!

What is interesting to me is these four words: 'build', 'pray', 'keep' and 'wait'. If you think about the inner life of a human being, it can be summed up under four headings: the mind (we think), the spirit (the real us), the will (we choose) and the heart (we feel). What Jude has been exhorting us to do speaks to every aspect of what we are inside. The mind: build yourselves up in your most holy faith — feed your mind. You are a living spirit: pray in the Spirit, your spirit and the Holy Spirit in communion — feed your spirit. The will: choose to walk in paths where you meet the love of God and where God is pleased to smile on you — keep yourselves in the love of God. And you have a heart; you have feelings. Many troubles break upon you, but keep your eyes on the love Christ has for you, and his coming, the consolation of eternal life that he brings — and so feed your affections. Here is a New Testament recipe for a healthy spiritual life even during times of trouble in the churches. We are not simply to sit back. We are to take responsibility for ourselves.

7.
Taking responsibility for others

Please read Jude 22-23

We are travelling through the book of Jude and we have nearly come to the end. We began the previous chapter by noticing that God intends men and women to be active. Christianity is not for spectators. It is a faith that tells us to participate, to be up and doing something. It is actually true that, although we learn as we hear the Word of God, we only really learn as we put it into practice. As we live out the Word, then new aspects of what God has said open up to us. Because we are now actually getting our hands dirty, as it were, in obeying God, we understand at a deeper level. So don't just read this commentary; genuinely seek to be active in putting what you learn into practice.

These verses 22-23 are sister verses to the previous pair of verses. In verses 20-21 we saw Jude telling us what we ought to be doing for ourselves as Christians. Now in these verses Jude is telling us what we as Christians ought to be doing for others.

The background is that there are false teachers threatening to cause severe damage to the churches. God will judge them. Now let me just remind you of the theme of the book. These false teachers have slipped into the churches and are saying that God is so gracious that once you are a Christian it no longer matters how you live. They are teaching that immorality is a viable option for the Christian. But Jude is vehemently rejecting this idea. Instead, by our words and by our lives, we must contend for the faith that was once for all entrusted to the saints (v. 4).

How is the ordinary church member to do that? First of all, Jude told us, in verses 20-21, that we must take responsibility for ourselves. We must build ourselves up in the true faith, so that we will not be deceived. We must be people of prayer. We must cling to Christ in personal faith and so keep ourselves in God's love. All the time we must keep our eyes on the fact that one day Christ will return, and so wait in hope.

But having told us, 'Take responsibility for yourselves,' now Jude is saying we must also take responsibility for other people: **'Be merciful to those who doubt; snatch others from the fire and save them; to others show mercy, mixed with fear — hating even the clothing stained by corrupted flesh'** (vv. 22-23).

He calls us to be up and doing as best we can in taking care of others: 'These are dangerous times for everybody, so be on the look-out for people and seeking to help.' The spirit of consumer society is very much: 'Look after yourself and others will have to look after themselves.' Such an attitude can rub off onto Christians in the churches as a type of spiritual self-ishness. But Jude is highlighting the fact that this is just the way to play into the hands of the false teachers and vacate the field to them. There are always lonely, needy, confused people both inside and around the edges of the church community. If serious Christians, who are concerned to uphold biblical stand-ards of doctrine and behaviour, do not get alongside and be-friend them, then be very sure that the false teachers and their followers will. It is just such vulnerable people that the devil loves to prey on. To neglect needy people is a sure way of allowing false teaching to get a hold of them and so have greater influence within the church as a whole. To look out for others is therefore a second practical step to be taken by ordinary Christians in contending for the faith.

To take responsibility for others will not always be comfortable. As in most areas of the Christian life, it will involve sacrifice. The story of General Gordon sets a simple but profound example. He was the nineteenth-century British soldier who won lasting fame, eventually losing his life in the defence of Khartoum. He served his country well but declined both a title and a financial reward offered to him by the British government. After some persuasion he accepted a gold medal inscribed with a record of his thirty-three military engagements and this medal became his most prized possession. After his death, however, it could not be found. It was only later, when his diaries were found, that it was discovered that, on hearing news of a severe famine, he had sent the gold medal to be melted down and used to buy bread for the poor. He had written in his diary, 'The last earthly thing I had in this world that I valued I have given to the Lord Jesus Christ today.' As a Christian man he wanted to do his best to take responsibility for others, following the example of his Saviour. Jude challenges us here in a different way to follow suit.

Once again, in these verses, we have Jude issuing us with four commands. We are to show mercy (v. 22). We are to show urgency: 'Snatch others from the fire' (v. 23). We are to show sensitivity: 'To others show mercy, mixed with fear' (v. 23). But, above all, we must show purity: 'hating even the clothing stained by corrupted flesh' (v. 23). As trouble and false teaching rage around the church, we must not only take care of ourselves but be active in seeking to help others. How? We find the answer by looking at these four commands.

Show mercy

First of all, we should show mercy: **'Be merciful to those who doubt'** (v. 22). Sometimes false teaching causes people to doubt. It can even cause good Christians of many years standing in Christ to doubt. New, false teaching sweeps in which opens up ideas that folk have never heard before and they begin to think, 'Have I been wrong? Could my Christian life have been so much better if only I had understood this new emphasis?' They are in a turmoil. They are in two minds.

Now that can be a dangerous situation, but it is not a sinful situation. Doubt is not the same as unbelief. Doubt is not a sin. Our response to such people who are in two minds should not be to cast them off. It should not be to say, 'Oh well, you fool, you must be a heretic, get out!' Some churches, of course, don't allow anyone to have any doubts or question anything. 'We know what we believe,' the leaders trumpet arrogantly. What happens then is that if people in the church do run into difficulty in their faith they keep their doubts to themselves. Their struggles remain hidden, for fear of what others might think of them. It is thought to be more spiritual just to accept whatever is said from the pulpit and never think through one's faith. And so those doubts fester. They are never dealt with and so these dear Christians become spiritually sick and weak. It can often be the case that the churches which are most proud of their doctrinal soundness harbour many ailing souls for this very reason. The reality has gone out of their faith because they do not feel able to face honest questions squarely. Now there is nothing wrong — indeed, there is everything right — with doctrinal soundness, but we are to beware of falling into such a superficial hold on our beliefs. Rather we are to be so confident in the truth of God and in his Word that we are quite happy for anyone to air questions.

'No,' says Jude. 'Our response to doubt is to be merciful.' That is, it is to be kind and understanding. We need to have an atmosphere in the church which is loving, so that people do feel that they can ask questions, that they can confess their fears and their doubts. Thus those doubts and fears are brought to the surface and they can be addressed. Those questions can be answered as we work in kindly fellowship together. That is how people can be brought out of confusion and know where they are going. They can come out of the other side of doubt with a stronger faith. A church where people fear one another, and where doubt is met with a harsh response, is a church where needy believers struggle alone. They are sitting targets for a false teacher with a warm handshake and a friendly demeanour. Be merciful to those who doubt.

Remember doubting Thomas, who had been with the Lord Jesus Christ and with the other disciples for three years. The others had seen the Lord alive from the dead on that first Easter Sunday, but when they told the absent Thomas about what had happened he doubted whether their claims were true. When the Lord Jesus heard those doubts of Thomas he could have said to himself, 'After three years of my being with him personally, he does not believe! I will leave him to his doubting.' But is that how the Lord Jesus reacted? Not at all. The Lord Jesus was not harsh when he heard those doubts of Thomas: 'Unless I see the nail-prints in his hands, I will not believe.' What does our loving Lord Jesus do? He appears to Thomas and he answers his doubts. He is gracious. He is merciful. We must follow in the Master's footsteps. 'Show mercy to those who doubt,' says Jude. Especially in days when false teaching is rampant, Christian, you have a responsibility in that area.

Show urgency

Secondly, we must show urgency: **'Snatch others from the fire and save them'** (v. 23). We have to be active in taking responsibility, not just for Christians inside the church, but for non-Christians outside the church too. We have a responsibility to evangelize.

Why has Christ left the church on earth when most things we do in the church could be done better in heaven? It is simply because we are left here as witnesses. People are on their way to a lost eternity. They are on their way to hell and they are unaware of it, blindly walking towards the abyss. And you and I have a responsibility: 'Snatch them from the fire.' The high priest Joshua in the prophecy of Zechariah was spoken of as a brand plucked from the burning. The reference is to Zechariah 3:1-5. The situation is possibly similar to that referred to in verse 9 if we understand that verse to mean that Satan accused Moses. Here Satan was standing to accuse the high priest of his sins. But the Lord rebuked Satan, and Joshua was given clean garments, symbolizing forgiveness, and so he is called 'a burning stick snatched from the fire'. Not to have our sins forgiven is to be exposed to the eternal fire. To be forgiven through the Lord Jesus Christ is to be snatched from the fire. That is one of the pictures here.

The great matter is that people *can* be saved. The destruction of Sodom and Gomorrah is a forewarning, said Jude in verse 7, of eternal fire. That is where non-Christian friends are bound, sadly. 'So do something about it!' Jude is saying. He is sounding an alarm and at the same time reminding us that God does rescue. We can have hope for our friends, but we must do something and we need to be urgent about it.

How do we get people to take us seriously? You only get people to take you seriously if you treat them in love, if you befriend them, if they know that you are not just treating them as some kind of evangelism fodder to get numbers into the church. How do people come to faith? So often it is through a Christian truly befriending them and then when the Christian shares the gospel, because they know that Christian well, because they have come to trust that person properly and know that he or she is an honest person, a man or woman of integrity, they take it seriously. In days when there are so many religions and false teachings going from door to door it is not surprising that non-Christians have many prejudices against the gospel. Do not get me wrong: there is nothing wrong with door-to-door work for the Christian, but try to see it from the non-Christian's point of view. Here is someone he does not know from Adam, arriving on his doorstep out of the blue, trying to foist upon him a set of religious ideas that seem very hard to swallow. Humanly speaking it is a non-starter. The non-Christian wants to see some proof that it is worth spending time taking this faith seriously. The best way of providing such proof is through a Christlike Christian life lived out in friendship before the eyes of our unconverted friends and neighbours. That is the way to win their attention and get a proper hearing for the gospel. We must be up and doing these things.

Think about Sodom and Gomorrah. When the angels came to save Lot with his family, you may remember, they asked Lot, 'Do you have anybody else here?' Lot then went to his sons-in-law and told them, 'The city is going to be destroyed,' but they took no notice. The Scripture says that it appeared to them that he was joking. So they stayed there and didn't take any notice of him and were destroyed in the judgement (Gen.19:12-14). Our non-Christian friends have got to see that we are serious about living holy lives if we are going to convince them that God hates sin. They have got to know that we truly love them if we are going to convince them that our God is a God of love, who saves sinners. They have got to see a Christian life that is not rooted in this world and the love of material things if we are going to convince them of eternal life and the world to come. We really do take eternal life seriously because Jesus really is risen from the dead as the Saviour of sinners. In other words, they have got to see a lifestyle that really does fit with the gospel.

Are you a saved person as you read these words? Please take this seriously. Jude is saying to us that the flames of eternal judgement are not imaginary. There is a fire to come. There is a judgement; that is why Jesus died. He died because there is a judgement on sin and he took the judgement himself for all who would believe in him. But all who will not believe in him must face the judgement themselves. If you are not yet Christ's, you need to be snatched from the fire. You need to open your heart to God and call upon him to save you, to bring you out. Take that seriously. Christ took it so seriously that he went to the cross for sinners. That is serious, isn't it? This is no joke. We must show urgency then, says Jude.

Show sensitivity

But, thirdly, we are not only to show mercy to those who doubt and urgency to those who are bound for the fire, but to show sensitivity too: **'To others show mercy, mixed with fear'** (v. 23). This seems almost like a combination of the previous two. By beginning with those words 'to others', it appears that here Jude has another separate category of people in view. He is probably thinking about those who have wandered from the Christian faith. Jude cares for the backsliders.

We can imagine that these people have been affected by the false teaching and so gone away from the Saviour. Perhaps they have been promised some ecstatic experience which will keep them on cloud nine for the rest of their lives, but it has not worked out like that. Perhaps they have been disappointed when the healing they were promised as a certainty, if only they exercised enough faith, failed to materialize. Perhaps they have heard some prosperity preacher making all kinds of promises about material wealth for them and those promises have not come true because they are not in the Bible. So because of such disappointments these people have rejected the whole thing. They have walked away from Christ and concluded that

Christianity is not true and decided to go back into the world. That kind of thing can happen, can't it?

Or perhaps they have succumbed to the kind of false teaching that Jude is opposing which turns the grace of God into a licence for immorality. Perhaps they have struggled with a certain sin for years, but the false teachers have convinced them that it is fine to pursue that sin openly and still be a Christian. They have followed that path, but found that the pangs of conscience would not be suppressed. Instead as they have come before God to pray their consciences have been red raw. Not being able to cope with this, they have wandered away from Christ in despair and given up all pretence of being Christians.

Backsliders go back into the world, out of the church. When Jude writes, 'To others, show mercy mixed with fear,' it seems to me that he has such people particularly in mind. When we approach those folk, we need to be very sensitive. There is a need to be merciful, but at the same time there is a need to show that the Lord is to be feared and is not someone to be trifled with. We need to be intelligent. We must not be all mercy, or all thunder, but sensitive to where they are as people, mixing mercy with fear. We are told to have mercy on them, to go and find them out. Do we go and find them out? Do we show them that we do still love them when they have left the church? Luke 15 tells of the shepherd who went and left the ninety-nine sheep and went after the lost one. Show them that you still love them. Don't look down on them because of what has happened to them, because there, but for the grace of God, go you and I.

Have mercy on them and pray that the Lord will give you the right words when you speak to them and when you see them, but mix that mercy with fear. Don't let them think that they are saved because they used to be in church once. Let them realize that it has to be a living, growing faith in the Saviour. That is the only true mark of real salvation and that they must repent and come back to him or they will be lost. So you need some bluntness and you need sensitivity to know the right way to do that. Of course, if you seek them out, some will refuse to see you. You cannot help that. You can only do your best. But if, in God's goodness, the backslider does listen and return to the church, then as a church receive him, forgive him, don't look down on him. Forgive and forget, and love him as the prodigal son was loved by the father when he returned. Don't be like that self-righteous elder brother who thought he was so good and was not pleased to see the prodigal return but, rather, was full of condemnation. Show mercy mixed with fear. 'Show sensitivity,' says Jude, and perhaps as we read these words faces come into our minds and names into our memories. If so, we need to love them.

However, the mention of fear may also be linked to what follows. We ourselves need to be careful. It is right that we should not be cocksure of ourselves. In rescuing those who have fallen we need to take heed and to fear falling ourselves. None of us is above becoming a backslider if we are not careful.

Show purity

So, as you take responsibility for others, showing mercy, showing urgency, showing sensitivity, above all, show purity: **'hating even the clothing stained by corrupted flesh'** (v. 23). We need to retain a godly hatred of sin.

The people you are trying to help need to see an honest, upright Christianity in you and, at the same time, you need to be careful. Doubters have been infiltrated by false ideas; take care that you are not infiltrated by them. Those who are non-Christians are often very much tied up with the world. Take care that you are not drawn into the world. Those backsliders may well tell you, 'Well, I have been where you are and the world is much better.' They *will* say that if Satan has got his grip on them at that particular moment. But you could be taken in and you can be hooked if you are not careful.

The phrase, 'hating even the clothing stained by corrupted flesh,' is a sort of metaphor for saying, 'Be very careful yourself, and realize that you need to get those people out of that uncleanness and back into the purity of Christ.' Paul warns us similarly in seeking to help those who have fallen: 'Brothers, if someone is caught in a sin, you who are spiritual should restore him gently. But watch yourself, or you also may be tempted' (Gal. 6:1). We have put off the old man and we must put on the new which is in Jesus Christ; we must live in the clean clothes provided by the Lord Jesus.

Commands for us all

So Jude has exhorted us to contend for the faith by taking responsibility for others. He has told us to show mercy, show urgency, show sensitivity and show purity. But the thing to understand is that this is not just addressed to pastors, is it? It is addressed to pastors but Jude does not say, 'Now, as I get to verse 22, I have got a special word for elders and pastors.' Such a statement just isn't there. We therefore have to infer that he intends this to be a call for us all as we take responsibility for one another. The church is a family. All the members of the family have a responsibility for other members. Yes, the elders have a special responsibility, but we all have a part to play. Here, then, are four key commands: mercy, urgency, sensitivity, purity. Let us try to draw a few conclusions.

The importance of the local church

First of all, from where is this ministry to be pursued? The obvious answer is that it is to be pursued from a local church.

Behind Jude's commands here is the assumption that all Christians should be committed to a definite congregation of God's people. You cannot take responsibility for the whole worldwide church. These commands apply to leaders but are not especially addressed to leaders. They apply to us all, and the assumption is that the Christians will take, as it were, ownership of their church. In one sense, of course, the church to which we are committed is not *our* church — perish the thought that it is! It is the Lord's church. But there is a right sense in which we should be able to say, 'This is my church.' We should be able to say it in the same way that we say, 'This is my father' or, 'This is my family.' I respect other people's families but my love and service are given to my own family. We cannot take responsibility for every Christian in all the world, or even in our own town, but we can take responsibility for our fellowship and those with whom our fellowship is in contact. That is God's will. Many people's attitude to the local church is the same as their attitude to the supermarket. They come in with the attitude: 'Have they got what I want? Well, if they haven't, I'll go to another one.' There is no sense of ownership. Would you do that with your family? You walk in and you see your family and think: 'Well, this is not very good, is it? I'll go to another one. The wife is looking a bit dowdy today. The kids are screaming. I think I'll find another one.' Yet that is the attitude that many people have to a church. That is all wrong.

Perhaps we are born into a church through conversion. In a special way, that is our church. Others perhaps have to move around the country with their job but they need to settle and decide: 'Yes, that's the place the Lord would have me be and that will be my church.' Without that ownership, the church wilts. If someone says, 'One church is just as good as any other for me; it makes no difference where I go,' then, as a general rule, that person never amounts to much in any church because he or she is always floating around and never getting really involved. Such people never accomplish much for God. So there is a real sense in which we should be able to speak of 'my church'. Jude's comments in verses 22-23 are really just another way of saying, 'Get involved in the life of your church.' This is the first conclusion from these commands.

The need for dedication

But then, secondly, we need to think not just *where* we are to fulfil these commands but a little more about *how*. How? If we are going to take seriously this matter of ministry and reaching out, we are going to need dedication. What Jude is exhorting us to do needs 'stickability,' because this is not an easy work.

I just love this story which underlines the kind of character we need. It is a true story, so far as I know, from the nineteenth century and it concerns a missionary candidate wanting to be involved in the Lord's work. He wanted to be out there snatching brands from the burning and helping God's people. He applied to a certain missionary society and it was decided that he would be interviewed by a great Christian leader of the day.

So the young man went to the Christian leader to fix a time for the interview. He was rather taken aback by the arrangement. The Christian leader said to him, 'Yes, come to my home next Saturday at 5 a.m.' The young man thought, '5 a.m.? How will I get there? There's no transport at that time of the day!' But he agreed. And he did get there. He walked there, and he arrived at 5 a.m. and rang the doorbell of the house. The leader opened the door, brought him in and sat him down in the hall and then went upstairs. He was not seen again until 7 a.m. Then he came down, walked past him in the hall and said, 'Wait there. I am just going to have my quiet time and get my breakfast.'

At 8.30 a.m., he came back to the young man, who was still there, and said, 'Come into my study, I want to ask you some questions.' Into the study went the young man and the missionary leader said to this young missionary candidate, 'I want to ask you about your education.' But the young man was astonished at the questions: 'How do you spell cat?' 'C-A-T', the young man replied. 'How about dog?' 'D-O-G.' 'What is three plus five?' 'Eight.' 'Fine,' said the Christian leader, 'off you go. Thank you very much for coming.' That was it. The young man went away wondering what on earth he had been doing.

But the Christian leader reported back to the missionary society and he explained what he had done. He had asked the candidate to arrive at 5 a.m. He had kept him waiting in the hall for hours. He had asked him questions about his education which were ridiculously simple. And he said, 'By doing that, I assessed that he had the three things that are necessary to really serve God and his people. By calling him to come at 5 a.m., I established that he had discipline. By leaving him in the hall for that long time and his not going away or getting upset, I established that he had patience. By asking him those silly questions about his education, I established that he had humility. He passed with top marks. I recommend this young man for the mission-field.'

Well, perhaps today we might want to ask a few more questions! However, the point is well made. Discipline, patience and humility — those are the prerequisites for true Christian service. Those are the prerequisites for showing mercy, snatching people from the burning and saving the backslider. We need to be sticking with that difficult job and not giving up.

8.
God is able!

Please read Jude 24-25

The theme of the closing verses of Jude is the exciting and joyful news that God is able. A few years ago a group of us who went to Kenya from our congregation one summer to take some Christian ministry had a powerful experience of that fact.

We were asked, through a friend, to go and take a conference for pastors and their wives from the African Inland Church, up in the wilds of Western Kenya, out in the country past the city of Kisumu. It is a part of the country which is poor and relatively neglected. When we were first asked to go on this trip, we knew how to fly from Britain to Nairobi, the Kenyan capital, but how would we get around after that? Our destination, the home of the AIC people on the shores of Lake Victoria, is a couple of hundred miles away from Nairobi. How would we find a place to rest and vehicles to go over the terrible roads? We thought of hiring a four-wheel-drive vehicle from a reputable company, but it was far too expensive. We wondered about approaching missionary friends to help us, but we were a party of seven people and the missionaries in Kenya have enough to do without suddenly having to look after us. The Christian folk to whom we were going are very poor and we did not want to be a burden to them. The situation just seemed to be impossible. There was nothing else to do but pray!

Very soon after we began to pray about this seriously, Pablo, one of our elders and part of the Kenya team, lost his job in a takeover of his firm. This seemed to add to our worries rather than help us and we wondered what the Lord was doing. For three months our brother kept having interviews, nearly getting new employment, but being passed over in the final interview. But eventually, with around seven months to go before we were due in Kenya, he landed a new position in a different company. This turned out to be God's amazing answer to our Kenya problems. On the first day at his new job Pablo was introduced to his new secretary. She was an African woman living in England. Eventually he asked her where she was from. 'Oh,' she replied, 'I am from near Kisumu in Kenya.' That made Pablo's ears prick up, as you can imagine. Conversation quickly turned to our conference trip and the problems we were facing. 'That is no problem,' she quickly said. 'My brother is a Christian. He used to be in the Kenyan Air Force and now he runs a travel business getting people around Kenya. He has cars and aircraft. He would be pleased to take care of all your arrangements at a price you can afford.'

Our jaws dropped open in astonishment when Pablo told us about all this. And it all worked out perfectly. The Lord had answered our prayers. The conference went ahead and the Lord provided in the most wonderful way. God is alive and he is in control — whatever he plans, he can finish. This is just one small example of that fact that 'God is able', the theme of the doxology which concludes the letter of Jude.

This is the reason for the praise: **'To him who is able to keep you from falling and to present you before his glorious presence without fault and with great joy — to the only God our Saviour, be glory, majesty, power and authority, through Jesus Christ our Lord, before all ages, now and for evermore! Amen'** (vv. 24-25). To God, who is able, be praise for all time!

Now this note of thankful praise is particularly relevant at the close of Jude's letter. Jude has written this epistle to counteract false teaching. The opening verses explained that certain men had secretly slipped in among the churches teaching that the grace of our God gave us a licence for immorality and that Jesus Christ was not our only Sovereign and Lord. Jude has written pungently, warning against these false teachers and the judgement which will certainly come upon them and those who follow them (vv. 4-19).

But while false teachers are pushing their poisonous doctrine and lifestyle, what must true Christians be doing? They must contend for the faith. For ordinary church members that means, first of all, taking responsibility for their own spiritual lives by building themselves up in the true faith, praying in the Holy Spirit, keeping themselves in the love of God and not despairing, but looking forward with hope to the Second Coming of the Lord (vv. 20-21).

But, secondly, they should be up and doing for others too. They must take responsibility for other people. Not to do so will play right into the hands of the false teachers. Christians must show mercy to those who doubt, show urgency in bringing the gospel to the lost, show sensitivity in seeking to regain backsliders and show purity in all this, especially as they work at a time when false teachers are encouraging immorality.

So this is what we must be busy doing. Now, as we come to the end of the letter, perhaps some people are saying to themselves, 'Well, I understand what you are saying, Jude, but this is a big job and a heavy responsibility. These false teachers are so subtle and many of them are so clever. Jude, how do I know that I won't be deceived? How can I be sure that I will walk the right path?' Jude replies, 'God is able. You don't have to live in anxiety. God is able to keep you.'

Meanwhile others may be thinking, 'Jude, you have told us that we must be up and doing, looking after ourselves and looking after others in the church. But Jude, I am tired. I am weary. Often I feel like giving up the fight. I am not sure that I can keep going.' Jude's answer is that 'God is able. The Lord has power for you. Put your hand in his hand and he will enable you to come safely home.'

Such questions are in the pastoral mind of the writer as he comes to the end of the letter. This is why Jude frames the concluding doxology of verses 24-25 in the way he does.

Praise is in Jude's heart. The contents of the verses can be divided simply into two sections. There is the reason for praising God and the expression of praise to God.

The rationale for praise to God

The reason for giving praise is that God is able. The sovereign God is joyfully able to do all his will. But Jude focuses on two aspects of that which are particularly pertinent to his readers. He is able to keep them and to present them faultless: **'To him who is able to keep you from falling and to present you before his glorious presence without fault and with great joy'** (v. 24).

He is able to keep us

First, then, he is able to keep us from falling. Christians are worried about all this false teaching and we can understand that they are worried about falling for it and its immorality themselves, and so falling away from Christ. But God is able to keep the Christian from falling away.

The idea of God keeping us from falling in verse 24 uses language borrowed from horse-riding. Riders jump fences and they go up steep slopes on their horses; they charge round the course and go through the rivers and over all kinds of obstacles.

In Britain we watch the Badminton horse trials each summer on TV and we all go, 'Oh!' when horses stumble and riders fall off. Yet the skilful rider manages to stay on and to keep the horse from stumbling. He or she manages to keep the horse in balance and guide it in the right way. What Jude is saying is that God is able to keep you from falling as if you were a horse and he were your rider. Christian, that rider on your back is the Lord Jesus Christ himself. He is holding the reins of your life and he is able to guide you and keep you from falling and to put you on the right track and bring you safely to heaven.

Now how does he do that? How does Christ keep us from falling? Let me suggest a number of practical ways in which this happens. How does Christ keep us from falling? I am sure there are more than the ways that I am going to suggest, but let me suggest a few of them.

First of all, Christ keeps us from falling *by his Word*. Has this ever happened to you, Christian? Perhaps you are facing great temptations, or great perplexity in your life, and it is with leaden steps that you come to church. God, as it were, drags you along. But, lo and behold, when you get there, the visiting preacher, who doesn't know anything about your situation, speaks from Scripture on the very matter that is causing you so much trouble. Light breaks upon you from God's Word. It is the word of God to your soul personally and you say to yourself, 'Well, I thought God had forgotten me. But he has known all about me all the time.' You are strengthened and heartened and you think, 'Even though I have been under such temptation the Lord has not cast me off. He loves me and knows all about me and I am going to carry on.' Has that ever happened to you? It has happened to me on many occasions and I am sure that it has happened to you as well if you are a Christian. He has kept us from falling.

Secondly, he keeps us not only by his Word but *by his Spirit*. Let me just say that I am dividing these two but, generally, we should not divide the Word and the Spirit; they usually very much go hand in hand. Have you ever got to the situation where you felt at the end of your tether? Perhaps other Christians have let you down, and you have been cut to the heart by their unhelpfulness. You felt so burdened and weak that you have, as it were, just fallen on your knees at your bedside and all that you have been able to say to the Lord is: 'Lord, aaahhhh!' And that was your prayer because you were so broken. That groan from the heart has indicated, 'Lord, I am in such trouble. I am angry and tired and I want to give up.' But as you have begun to groan in prayer, somehow or other, a strength has welled up within you; a peace has come up on your soul; a light has shone into your mind. It is the Holy Spirit within you. Somehow or other, you have been given new strength to go on by his Spirit. He is able to keep you from falling.

God also keeps us from falling *by his providence* and *by his church*. Imagine yourself in the position of someone who is determined that he or she has had enough of the Christian faith. You are going to walk out on Christ and you are going to go into the world and to give yourself to all its temptations. You have had enough and you are walking out. It is Friday or Saturday night and you are going out. But just as you are about to leave the house, there is a phone call and it is a Christian friend. It has come at just that moment and you realize that someone does love you. God's family does care. That call changes the whole situation. It could have been five minutes later and you would have gone out of the door and would not have heard the phone. But in God's providence, that phone call comes. Or perhaps you have met someone from church on the way and somehow that is the very person you have been able to open up to with your troubles. Just the love of others has buoyed you up. God has sent that particular person just at that time and he has kept you. God keeps us by his Word, by his Spirit, by his providence, by his church.

Here is another way God keeps us from falling: *by his angels*. This seems particularly appropriate to mention, given Jude's interest in angels. I cannot claim great understanding of this, but it is in the Scriptures. Hebrews 1:14 tells us that there are angels who are 'ministering spirits sent to serve those who will inherit salvation'. They watch over us, and God uses them.

One story on this subject has always encouraged me. The eighteenth-century preacher and hymn-writer Philip Doddridge recounted a remarkable dream. He tells how that many things had happened in his life which he had never understood. He speaks of circumstances that had worked out which at the time had amazed him. There were incidents in which he was sure he was going to be injured but, somehow, it didn't happen. He tells us that one night he had a dream. He dreamed that he died. He saw himself looking down on his funeral and he was taken to heaven. In heaven he was shown to a great mansion. Doddridge says that in the dream he entered and the angel said, 'Wait here and the Lord will come and see you.' As he entered the mansion he began to walk around. He entered a large room, and he saw that around the walls of the room was an intricate mural. As he looked at it, he realized that it actually depicted the story of his life. He could see himself as a young boy and then as an older man. But as he looked, he saw many of those incidents in his life where exceptional things happened and he had not understood how he had escaped harm. At those places in the mural, to his surprise, he saw angels. The angels were there.

Now that is Philip Doddridge's dream. Make of it what you will. But the Scriptures assure us plainly that there are angels who watch over us, ministering spirits sent by the Lord to care for his people, including you and me. It was an angel who was sent to the Lord Jesus Christ when he was agonizing in the garden of Gethsemane. It was partly the strength given by that angel which enabled him to carry on with God's will and not shy away from the cross. The angels care for us too. That is another way that God is able to keep us from falling.

The final way is perhaps a more strange way. Let me put it like this: God is able to keep us from falling *by letting us fall temporarily.* He is able to keep us from falling — in other words, walking out on him — by letting us fall temporarily. Sometimes it seems that the Lord does let us fall momentarily into sin so the taste of that evil thing is so bitter that we will never do it again.

We can think of a great example of this in the case of Simon Peter. Do you remember his protests on the night that Jesus was betrayed? 'Though everyone else should forsake you, I will not. Though everyone else walks out on you, I'll stay with you, Lord. I'll even die for you.' There he was with his pride, his self-reliance, his arrogance, and that needed to be broken; otherwise he would make a shipwreck of his Christian faith. What did Christ do? He allowed him to fall. Christ was arrested. Peter followed. They were in the courtyard. People came up to Peter and challenged him: 'You were with Christ. You were with Jesus.' Peter was afraid. He declared, 'I never knew him.' Peter denied his Lord. While this was going on in the courtyard, the Lord Jesus was just across the courtyard on trial, and the Lord turned and looked straight at Peter. Then Peter remembered the words the Lord had spoken to him: 'Before the cock crows today, you will disown me three times.' We are then told in Scripture that Peter went outside and wept bitterly. He was broken by the experience. He was allowed to fall, but the taste of it was so bitter that he never denied the Lord again. The Lord accepted him back and he would not deny him again. Later, we know from church history, Peter was prepared to die for the Lord. It was such a bitter thing when the Lord looked at him that it broke Peter's heart. He is able to keep us from falling by allowing us to fall temporarily.

But here is the assurance. Christians, faced with trials and temptations, you are not to live in anxiety. He is able to keep you in these ways and in many others. There is an application here too for the person who is not yet a Christian. If you are a non-Christian wavering on the brink of coming to Christ but saying to yourself, 'I'd love to be a Christian, but I don't think I could keep it up,' here is the assurance that he is able to keep you from falling — so come to him.

So Jude is praising God first of all that he is able to keep us. Isn't that wonderful? Even though we may not have had many remarkable or startling occurrences in our Christian lives, here is a continual reason to praise the Lord. Are we going on with Christ? If we are, it is because God is keeping us. Then let us worship and thank him.

He is able to present us

The second reason which stirs Jude to praise is that God is able to present us faultless. Our verse tells us that God **'is able to keep you from falling and to present you before his glorious presence without fault and with great joy'**. Jude assures Christians that God is able to present us faultless in heaven, in glory.

The words 'to present' are words that come from the background of an Old Testament sacrifice being offered, or presented, to God to honour him. The offerings of the temple were presented to the Lord. Jude is telling us that God is able to present us to himself, faultless. We ourselves in heaven, our lives as living sacrifices (Rom.12:1-2) and our persons in heaven, are presented to the Lord. It is right to ask a question at this point: why is Jude speaking in these terms? Why is he using that kind of imagery as he looks towards heaven?

The answer probably resides in the nature of the false teaching Jude is opposing. What is the crux of what the heretics are offering? They turn the grace of God into a licence for immorality and sin. The nub of it is that once God has saved you, you can live as you like. The crux of it is to have eternal life and be able to live for self. It is a man-centred gospel. But in this imagery of presenting a sacrifice to God, Jude is striking at the very heart of this idea. He is saying, 'Salvation is about being saved and forgiven, that your life may be presented, not to yourself, but to God. Salvation centres on God. It is about the fact that, through Jesus Christ, your life may be a sacrifice, pleasing to the Lord, being presented to him.' So he is using this imagery to once again put a hammer blow through this false teaching. Real Christianity is about salvation to the glory of God. In true conversion, our lives are turned around, away from self and towards pleasing God. If that has not happened, there is no true salvation.

However, having said that, although that is where a true Christian's desire is, we are very much aware that we are not yet perfect as Christians. We are aware that we fail the Lord so often, although we want to live for him. Jude's second source of praise is that though now we are not yet perfect, God is able to present us faultless with great joy then. He will present you, if you are a Christian, without fault, to himself, through Christ. The cross of Jesus pays for all our sins. His perfect life of righteousness clothes us. So we are made totally pleasing to God.

Let me use an example which may be helpful here. The work of an editor provides a vivid illustration of presenting a life perfect to God. Think about the father of faith, the life of Abraham. If you read the life of Abraham in Genesis, you will find that there are many failings, many sins, many times when he lets the Lord down. He trusts God to go to the promised land, but in times of famine he runs to Egypt and trusts his own wisdom. He believes God will give him a son, but then goes along with the idea of using his wife's maid to provide him with an heir. There are numerous failings. But then you read the life of Abraham again in Hebrews 11. It is very different. None of those sins is there. None of his failings is mentioned. They have all, as it were, been under the editor's red pen, and edited out. Abraham is perfect. The heavenly editor has made his life just right through the blood of Christ.

All our failings are covered, and we are taken up and clothed in Christ's righteousness. Like Abraham we are made perfect before the Lord. And the Lord is greatly pleased as we arrive in heaven. We are not just tolerated: 'Oh yes, please come in and stand over there.' That is not the greeting we receive. The Lord is pleased and welcomes us with great joy: 'Come in, my sons, my daughters, come into my presence. I love you!' The Lord is full of great joy to see his plans in Christ fulfilled.

And, you know, part of that joy of God, it seems to me, will flow out of the troubles we faced for him on earth. Think about soldiers who have fought a war. Who are the ones that are given the medals? Is the Victoria Cross given to those who have been at the back looking after the supplies and have never been anywhere near the action? Is the Distinguished Service Medal awarded to those who have sat behind desks at headquarters, miles from the front line? The medals are given to those who have been right in the thick of battle, where the explosives have been going off and where it has been really tough. Similarly with great joy, God will, as it were, pin the Victoria Cross on those who have been through the trouble, through the fire, for him, and will own them before the whole universe. With great joy, he will declare, 'These are my sons, my daughters, now and for ever. They did all this for me.' So God is glorified and we are blessed.

There is a particular verse which aptly summarizes the fact that our present troubles bring future blessing. 2 Corinthians 4:17 is a verse to latch on to. Paul, the writer, was a great soldier for the Lord Jesus Christ. He was a hero of the faith, often beaten, stoned, rejected and slandered in the battle. What does Paul say? 'For our light and momentary troubles [he is being ironic] are achieving for us an eternal glory that far outweighs them all.' Those troubles are not something by the way. They are not vaguely linked to the glory of heaven. Our troubles, including having to contend for the faith against false teaching, are achieving for us an eternal glory that far outweighs them all — a great weight of glory. Part of the joy will come from the troubles that we have suffered for Christ. He is able to present us faultless and with great joy.

The expression of praise to God

Having alluded in verse 24 to how marvellously God keeps us and perfects us, Jude concludes with directing praise to God: **'To the only God our Saviour be glory, majesty, power and authority, through Jesus Christ our Lord, before all ages, now and for evermore! Amen'** (v. 25).

It is worth spending a little time and analysing this doxology under three headings.

The description of God

He is described as **'the only God'**. That the God of Israel was the only true God was the distinctive Jewish confession of faith. Jude is writing, almost without doubt, to Jewish Christian communities. He would be reminding them of their roots by this expression and also underlining that apostolic Christianity stands full square with the solid monotheism of the Old Testament revelation. Perhaps the false teachers he is opposing saw themselves in some ways as 'masters' or 'gods'. Jude is highlighting the horrible incongruity of such ideas in the light of Scripture. In our own day, we face the ever-increasing call for a syncretistic world-faith which can embrace all religions. The demand is for a composite God whose identity somehow includes any and every view of what God is like. But the New Testament tells us there is but one true God, who has revealed himself in and **'through Jesus Christ our Lord'**. Our worship is to be sharply focused on him alone.

God is also described as **'our Saviour'**. Again, this is a traditional Jewish term for God, paraphrasing the idea of 'the God of our salvation'. In the light of the false teaching Jude is opposing, this is a timely reminder that even as Christians we still need a Saviour. We have not been saved in such a way that we no longer need the Lord. We do not have strength in ourselves. As verse 24 reminded us, we continually need him to keep us from falling and to go on to bring us to heaven. In the unity of the Trinity, God himself has become our Saviour in every possible way. The Father has called us to himself (v. 1). The Son, Jesus Christ, has died and risen from the dead as our representative, and in him we are kept safe (v. 1). The Holy Spirit changes our hearts (v. 19) and enables us to pray and receive the strength and grace the Lord provides (v. 20).

The nature of the doxology

Jude proclaims that **'glory, majesty, power and authority'** are to go to God. The choice of words here is interesting. Apart from perhaps the first word in the series, all of the words carry the connotation of being subject to God. They are words which are used of a king, or one who rules. This expression of praise, then, is specifically an expression of submission to God. It is a proclamation that it is right that God should command us and that all should subordinate themselves to him.

'*Glory*' speaks of a concern for the fame and adulation of God. '*Majesty*' gives a sense of the transcendent sovereignty of God. '*Power*' speaks of the unrivalled strength and force of God. And to ascribe power to him is to rejoice in the fact that all heaven and earth are under his sway and to condemn all who would seek to oppose him. '*Authority*' is an ascribing of the right to use power.

There are other nuances in other biblical doxologies. In Revelation the company of heaven cries, 'Worthy is the Lamb!' The word 'worthy' would have been used by the crowd in acclaiming an athlete who had won a vital victory. The praise would focus on the achievement of the one being praised. This doxology is slanted more towards the idea that the one being praised should be worshipped through submission to him. Again, in view of the self-centred and antinomian nature of the heresy which Jude is opposing, this form of doxology seems to have been carefully chosen. The doxology calls us away from the boasting language (v. 16) and the rejection of authority (v. 8) which are characteristic of the false teachers. It steers us towards humility and thankful obedience. These are the things we should give to God.

The time reference

When should we give these things, and when should these things be ascribed to God? What is the time-scale of his praise, according to Jude? His answer is mind-boggling. He takes us back before the beginning of time: **'before all ages'**. Then Jude tells us to ascribe glory to the Lord **'now'**. Then he goes on to declare that God is to be worshipped **'for evermore'**.

This threefold reference to past, present and future is unique in Jewish and early Christian doxologies. Normally there is a reference to the present and the future, but Jude refers us back into eternity past as well. This is probably another way of subtly underlining the uniqueness and pre-eminence of the Lord Jesus Christ. The false teachers denied him as the only Sovereign and Lord. But Jude turns our attention to the praise of God and astutely raises the question of how God was praised before all ages. Yes, there were angelic beings, but the Scriptures plainly state that they are not eternal beings. They were created. Before their creation, how was God praised? Jude tells us that he was, within the unity of the Trinity, given **'glory, majesty, power and authority, through Jesus Christ our Lord, before all ages'**. Here is the uniqueness of Jesus Christ. He is eternally one with the Father, and eternally the one through whom glory is brought to the Father. There is no one, angelic or human, who can compare with him. Thus again, in this doxology, the foolish pretensions of the false teachers are being punctured.

That is, how, when, and why should we give the praise to God. We should worship him because he is unique, the only God. History is the outworking of the proof that everything else is false, except the Christian God. That is what history is really about. Other gods rise and fall. False teachings and political ideologies will have their day. But they will fail. He is the only God our Saviour. He is the one who loves the weak and the needy. He is the one who loves sinners and alone has given himself for sinners in Jesus Christ. There is no one like him. There is no love like his love. That is why we submit to him and ascribe to him the power, the majesty, the glory and the authority before all ages, now and for evermore.

How should that praise be given to him? Not just in any way we like, but through Jesus Christ our Lord, who is the only way to God. It is the true teaching which comes through Jesus, God's own Son, which enables us to know God and worship him according to his will.

Submission to God

In many ways, as we have already mentioned, the slant which Jude puts on the doxology at the end of the letter brings to a head the vital difference between the false religion of the heretics and the true faith of the New Testament church. In closing the letter it is worth meditating on this. The false teachers were arrogant people, who rejected authority (v. 8) and were in many ways a law unto themselves. They saw redemption in terms of self-fulfilment and self-promotion (v. 16), in other words reaching some stage of spiritual life where they could do whatever they wanted. Ironically and by contrast, true salvation is found in precisely the opposite direction. It is found in repentance and submissive trust and obedience to the God who loves us. In many ways this is the main thrust of Jude's epistle which calls us to contend for the faith.

We do well, therefore, to remind ourselves of the blessings of obedience to the sovereign God of love. The Bible uses the picture of a potter and the clay to illustrate something of the relationship between the Lord and his people. Someone has taken that metaphor and expanded it into a useful parable to underline the blessing of obedience.

Imagine six lumps of clay which the master potter wants to mould into flowerpots on his wheel and then they are to be fired in the kiln and made useful to people.

But the first lump of clay said, 'I don't need any master potter. I'll make myself into a strong, attractive flowerpot by my own strength.' He is still trying.

The second lump said to the potter, 'I want to be really big and impressive; make me as big as you can.' The trouble was that he was only the same size as the other lumps, so to be made large he had to be made with very thin walls. He was too fragile and broke before he was even fired.

The third lump saw what had happened to the second lump and laughed. 'I don't want to be big,' she said. 'I want to be beautiful. I want to be covered in designs and patterns and painted.' So she was. But nobody would buy her, for somehow she didn't look right for a working flowerpot.

The fourth lump was made on the wheel, but was afraid to go into the kiln. 'Please don't put me in there,' she said. 'It is so unbearably hot and painful.' So she was left behind in the shed and never saw the light of day.

The fifth lump was not frightened of the kiln, but was rather dirty and impure. He went without concern into the fire. Yet in the kiln the temperature was so hot that the impurities deep within him cracked him wide open and he broke to pieces.

The sixth lump, however, was happy to trust the potter and to go through whatever purifying, shaping and firing processes he thought necessary. As a result she was a solid specimen, of immense usefulness and was always full of wonderful flowers.

It is a simple parable, but it leads us in the right direction. In our day there are thought to be many ways to God from which a person can choose. In our day, in which every emphasis is put upon self, insisting on our 'rights' and getting what we want, the deviant heresies of Jude's false teachers still have their contemporary counterparts, both inside and outside the church. But salvation lies in submitting our hearts and lives to 'the only God our Saviour' (v. 25) and to 'Jesus Christ our only Sovereign and Lord'(v. 4).

Here, in Jude's great statement that God is able, we are to find our peace even in troubled times. Not only will he save us and bring us safe into his presence, but he will also uphold his plans and preserve his church and his gospel. Whatever the opposition from outside, whatever the confusion inside the church, he is able. As we said at the beginning of this book, there are times when there is so much error and there are so many enemies that the gospel seems like a lost cause. But God is able, and those who write off the Christian faith will always find that they have spoken too soon.

The words of the twentieth-century novelist G. K. Chesterton are worth remembering. He said something like this: 'Christianity has died many times and risen again; for it has a God who knew the way out of the grave. And often the faith has to all appearances gone to the dog. In each case it was the dog that died.'

9.
The relevance of Jude today

At the turn of the second millennium we have to confess that the church in the Western world appears at a low ebb. This may not be true elsewhere in the world, but Europe and the United States are rapidly becoming post-Christian societies.

The prevailing outlook of our time, which is the driving force behind this move away from Christian civilization, is subjectivism.

The secular form of this subjective introversion is the so-called post-modern mind-set. With the old certainties of the benefits of God and destiny, science and rationalism in doubt, everything is seen as relative. All that matters is the way an individual feels and the way he or she sees things. Image counts, but the claim that we can know absolute truth is dismissed as ridiculous. Feelings matter, but if morality gets in the way of personal enjoyment then so much the worse for morality.

The religious form of this introversion is the New Age movement. It is the ultimate in spiritual pluralism. This is a composite collection of religious ideas, mostly from the East and the occult, which again focuses on the individual, who is free to choose some aspects and reject others. It offers personal power and emotional integration through spiritual experiment and encounter.

Both of these subjective approaches to life therefore focus on the experiential and the therapeutic. All forms of authority outside the individual are rejected. We live in a time when individual stimulation is everything. So people are hooked on the visually impressive and on the sensually decadent. In such an environment, a church whose influence seems to be dwindling is in a very vulnerable state. It is under threat in two ways.

Firstly, it is in danger of *compromise with the world*. Tired of swimming against the tide of permissiveness, despised as starchy and moralistic by the surrounding decadent fun-culture, the church can be tempted to throw away its commitment to biblical standards of behaviour and gain popularity by going with the flow. Tired of swimming against the flood of pluralism and the teaching that 'All religions lead to God', written off as bigoted and narrow, the church is tempted to ditch its commitment to the uniqueness of Christ as the only Lord in the quest for social acceptability. It is difficult to be clear and holy in a pluralistic and unholy world. But if the church loses the truth of the gospel and its holiness, it loses the presence of the Lord and comes under his displeasure.

But secondly, it is in danger from *ecstatic heretics*. With the church in difficulty, there has sprung up a deep desire in the hearts of many Bible-believing Christians to see revival and the power of God visiting the churches again. Much of this desire is sincere and firmly founded in love for Christ. Some of it is less worthy and has more to do with dented pride and being seen to be part of an 'unsuccessful' church in an image-conscious world. In desperation to see revival there is a grave risk that Christians will be open to accept anything that has the appearance of the supernatural about it, even if it departs from the biblical gospel. We can be ready to go with anything that causes a sensation and attracts a crowd. We long to be seen to be successful. This second danger is especially heightened in a post-modern environment in which the 'feel-good factor' and public relations are everything and truth is at a discount.

As we read the epistle of Jude, we find that the writer is combating false teaching which is a vicious and intriguing mixture of these two threats to the contemporary church.

Here we find heretical teachers infiltrating the church who claim to receive heavenly revelations (v. 8), who teach things contrary to the apostolic faith (v. 4), who do not see Jesus as the only Lord (v. 4), who are highly motivated and plausible (v. 16) and who speak vividly and arrogantly of supernatural encounters with celestial beings (vv. 8-9). There is plenty of excitement here and plenty of sensational images. Yet at the same time these false teachers are people who encourage sexual sin within the church. They see themselves as an élite and preach that it is right for them to be a law unto themselves, under no authority (v. 8). 'They are godless men, who change the grace of our God into a licence for immorality and deny Jesus Christ our only Sovereign and Lord' (v. 4).

In many ways Jude's heretics encapsulate all the worst dangers to the church and the biblical gospel today. The letter of Jude therefore, is a tonic and a prescription for our times.

Contending for the faith

Though Jude has the dignity of being a half-brother of the Lord Jesus Christ, in contrast to the arrogance of the heretics, he introduces himself only as Christ's servant (v. 1). If we seek to battle for the truth, a humble attitude is the only one which will commend Christ, who humbled himself to death on the cross for our salvation.

As he begins his letter, our writer immediately clarifies for us the crucial question of 'What is a Christian?' Unless we know the genuine we cannot counter the forgery. Over against the false teachers who frame salvation in terms of attaining personal autonomy and sensual gratification, Jude's definition of a Christian is God-centred. We are those who are called, loved and kept by our Lord and Master (vv. 1,4). Further, in an experience-crazy world, Jude does not reject religious experience, but explains that true Christianity consists of the experience of God's mercy, peace and love. Apostolic Christian experience is focused, not on spiritual or physical ecstasy, but on the felt knowledge of sins forgiven issuing in a life of love.

The central feature of Christianity, for which we must fight, is 'the faith that was once for all entrusted to the saints' (v. 3). The fundamentals of the Christian faith are not open to ongoing revision, whether from the pressures of the changeable world or from ephemeral charismatic communications. God has spoken in his Son Jesus Christ, accurately and finally. The truth has been delivered to the church in the Scriptures of the Old and New Testaments. Salvation by the grace of God, the lordship of Jesus Christ and the distinctive nature of the Christian life as a holy and moral life are totally non-negotiable. We may need to translate these central teachings to make them understandable to people of different cultures and different times, but we must never change them. Rather, we must contend for them against anything which opposes them. The test of spirituality is always loving, humble, moral rectitude, in submission to Jesus Christ as Master and Lord. This cannot be stressed often enough in a post-modern/New Age environment which sees ethical behaviour as relative.

The wrath of God

In facing temptation to slide morally and doctrinally, Jude finds it most urgent to warn Christians and churches of the wrath of God. If we truly belong to Jesus Christ, we are safe for time and eternity because by the grace of God our sins are forgiven. We are kept by Jesus Christ. But no one who has truly received the grace of God will feel able to use his liberty to indulge self and pursue sin. Those that do show themselves not to have been truly the Lord's people at all. Such will suffer eternal judgement (v. 7). At a practical level, no one can be so sure of being saved that he, or she, can afford to throw off restraint.

Jude has used three well-known Old Testament stories to drive this lesson home. Many of those Israelites who were saved out of bondage in Egypt died in the desert because of their unbelief and rebellion (v. 5). Even angelic beings are not exempt from God's judgement if they will not obey (v. 6), so let none of us think that we are above such strictures and that this warning does not apply to us. The cities of Sodom and Gomorrah, which gave themselves over to sexual immorality, are a standing example of the judgement of God of which everyone needs to take heed (v. 7). It has been well said by many faithful preachers that if God does not judge the immorality of our own time he will have to apologize to the people of those ancient cities. His judgement is certain.

We live in days when talk of God's wrath is unfashionable and looked upon with distaste. This too is partially a result of our post-modern, self-indulgent culture, with its therapeutic understanding of what is 'good' having replaced the biblical emphasis that 'goodness' has a moral dimension. 'A good God would not hurt anyone,' we are told. In our vanity we cannot see anything more precious than a human being. Though human beings are precious, there are things which are more precious. Our God prizes love over lust; he prizes his own integrity over the approval of a fallen public. Christian minds can be too much influenced by the prevailing spirit of the times. We are not to think that talk of God's righteous anger is to be stored in the theological attic, as bric-a-brac from bygone days. God is unchanging. God is not only loving; he is holy and has a deep antipathy to all that is sinful. He had it in the days of Sodom and Gomorrah and he still has it today. Therefore the church is to take Jude's warnings with deadly seriousness.

Arguing against heresy

The teaching of the false teachers was such as to deny the lordship of Christ and therefore the authority of his Word over them. Because of this, Jude feels that to make progress against the heresy he must first argue against the false teachers using their own favoured literature. Though, as Jews, Jude's readers would acknowledge the Old Testament, it is no good quoting the teaching of the Lord Jesus to many of those who have been influenced by the heretics, for they do not recognize his authority. This is probably the explanation of why Jude uses the inter-testamental writings, *The Assumption of Moses* and *The Book of Enoch.*

This is a pointer to us that in arguing for Christ in the contemporary world, we need not only to know our Bibles, but also to join the battle of ideas with our opponents on their own ground. We believe that Christ alone is the truth and therefore all other philosophies, religions, spiritual teachings and world-views are ultimately incoherent. Jude is not prepared simply to quote the Bible if he feels that there are barriers to its reception. He goes over into enemy territory and makes his point from there. We must follow Jude in our day where this is necessary. This is a vast task in our complex contemporary world, and therefore specialist Christian apologists have a place in today's church. They must work very hard and we must pray to God for them.

In particular Jude quotes from *The Assumption of Moses* to show that, rather than being a wise élite, the false teachers are spiritually ignorant (vv. 8-10). Then he uses *The Book of Enoch* to bring encouragement to faithful Christians who may be despondent at the apparent success of heresy. God has always known of these men and long ago their condemnation was proclaimed (vv. 14-15). The apostles through whom Jude's readers first heard the gospel explained that the battle with derisive opponents of the truth is normal for the last days in which the church lives (v. 18). The implication is that we are not to despair as we face false teaching. Though there is much to grieve about, we are to realize that God is in control.

This too is a note which needs to be sounded among faithful evangelicals. As we see the latest deviation from biblical Christianity, whatever it may be, influencing many in the churches, we can become grim and harsh, and the joy of Christ can evaporate from our churches. This is hardly glorifying to the Lord, nor does it help the cause of truth. We can let the latest trouble for the churches fill our horizon and get things out of perspective. We can become so entrenched in battling for the truth that we neglect our personal relationship with the Lord Jesus who is the truth. Rather our grasp of the sovereignty of God should be such that, though we lament over false teaching and false teachers, at the same time we can still enjoy our Saviour and our salvation. The best way to commend the true gospel is through holy lives lived in happy fellowship with Jesus.

Taking responsibility

Jude's epistle then moves on to stir up ordinary Christians to action.

First of all, he calls us to take responsibility for our own spiritual lives (vv. 20-21). False teaching is dangerous. Every Christian must look to himself or herself. We are to study to build ourselves up in our most holy faith, understanding the truth which Scripture has given. We are to be people of prayer, bringing ourselves and the needs of the church to the Father, through Jesus Christ, in the Spirit. We are to keep ourselves in the love of God, both seeking the Lord's approval and fanning into flame our own love for him. We are to be those who live in hope, waiting for the coming of the Lord. Obviously, church leaders have the responsibility of caring for their flocks, but in times when he has to be fighting false teachers, the church leader's job is made much easier if solid Christians are looking out for themselves. If a shepherd knows that the ninety-nine can be relied on to look after themselves for a while, he feels much freer to go looking for the one who has strayed.

Secondly, Jude encourages us all, not only to look out for ourselves, but to try to take responsibility for others (vv. 22-23). He tells us that we must tenderly care for those who fall into doubt, we must be robust in our reaching out to the lost who are in danger of hell and we must be wise in the way we go after backsliders and try to bring them back to God's fold. In all this we must humbly watch ourselves, knowing that, as fragile sinners without the Lord's strength, we could fall for the temptations of this world.

The note which must not be missed here is this. The trumpet call of Jude's letter is to 'contend for the faith'. But what we find here at the everyday level is that contending for the faith actually means contending for people. We must look out for our own souls. We must look out for the souls of others. Frequently contending for doctrine can become doctrinaire. Those who are valiant for truth have often done the truth a great disservice in failing to care for people. 'If you do not toe the party line, then you can go!' There is no humanity, we could say no real Christianity, about such an attitude, especially when it is adopted towards those who may be young in the faith or who have genuine questions which trouble them. We shall only communicate the faith and defend it worthily as the truth is mixed with love. It is worth reflecting that many false teachers come to prominence as they pick up on the lonely and the needy who have been passed over by more orthodox Christians.

Helpful as books are, contending for the faith is not accomplished by writing books. That books and tracts are necessary is obviously seen from the fact that Jude felt moved to write. But he exhorts his readers not to be content with having the truth in a book, or even grasping the content of the faith in their own minds. It must overflow into a personal walk with Christ, fired by the Holy Spirit. It must move us to battle for the souls of others, longing to see them sound in the faith, safe for time and eternity and enjoying their own relationship with Christ. Contending for the faith, therefore, is not simply an intellectual or academic exercise. It is an exercise of the heart in feeling for those led astray. It is an exercise of the will, and indeed of the body, in choosing to be up and doing for the love of our friends in the church and beyond.

Our post-modern/New Age society tells us we need only care for ourselves. Subjectivism is about self. At the same time our age is also materialistic. These influences tend to make us introverted and lazy. If we are, the false teachers will continue to have a field day. We must regain Jude's vision of contending for the faith, not just at the intellectual level, but at the level of practical, loving Christianity for those led astray.

Jude finishes on a triumphant note. The battle with false teaching which legitimizes immorality is a dangerous and hard battle. But God is able. We are not to be gloomy or despondent. As we co-operate with the Lord, biblical Christianity will conquer. Our God is sovereign and is able to accomplish all his will, which includes bringing you and me, Christian, safe to the joyous presence of God in heaven.

Select bibliography

Michael Green, *2 Peter & Jude,* Tyndale Commentary, IVP, 1977.

Dick Lucas & Chris Green, *The Message of 2 Peter & Jude,* Bible Speaks Today, IVP, 1995.

Richard J. Bauckham, *Jude & 2 Peter,* Word Biblical Commentary, Word Publishers, 1983.

The Book of Enoch, English translation by Matthew Black, E. J. Brill, Leiden, Holland, 1985.

The Assumption of Moses, A critical edition with commentary by Johannes Tromp, E. J. Brill, Leiden,1993.

Christopher Hill, *The World Turned Upside Down,* Penguin, 1991.

Hank Hanegraaf, Christianity in Crisis, Harvest House, USA, 1993.

Hank Hanegraaf, *Counterfeit Revival,* Word Publishing USA, 1997.

Peter Jones, *Spirit Wars,* Winepress Publishing USA, 1997.

Peter Graystone, *Ready Salted,* Scripture Union, 1998.

Simon Coupland, *A Dose of Salts,* Monarch Publications, 1997.